Praise for FLOWERS ARE FOREVER

"Everyone loves flowers! Let the inspiration in this book touch your heart deeply!"

—KAY ALLENBAUGH, AUTHOR OF THE NATIONAL BESTSELLING *Chocolate for a Woman's Soul* SERIES

"If you love flowers, you will love this garden of stories, vignettes, and floral wisdom. As I read the stories, I could see the beautiful blooms and smell their fragrance. But best of all, I experienced how the beauty of flowers touches the human heart."

—ANN HIBBARD, AUTHOR AND SPEAKER

"Flowers are with us throughout life. They greet the newborn; crown the victor; persuade the beloved; celebrate the birthday and holiday; beautify the wedding; glorify the church; congratulate the anniversary couple and finally express emotions too difficult for words when they stand as loving memorials at the funeral wake... Kathy Lamancusa has compiled stories that will in some way resonate in all of us."

—BILL HIXSON,
FOUNDER OF THE INTERNATIONAL FLORAL DESIGN SCHOOL

"Excellent... written with humor and feeling."

—JOE MAIDEN, HOST OF *Grow with Joe* (THE LEARNING CHANNEL) AND *Grow Your Own* (THE DISCOVERY CHANNEL)

"Touching, beautiful stories which artfully express the effect flowers have on the human spirit. Flowers Are Forever *reminds each of us that flowers constantly interpret our emotions and serve to remind us of how the soul of a flower triumphs, by enlightening the heart with hope, happiness, and love."*

—HOLLY MONEY-COLLINS, AIFD,
PROFESSOR OF ENVIRONMENTAL HORTICULTURE AT CITY COLLEGE OF SAN FRANCISCO

" 'Flower soup' for the soul! With numerous stories, essays, quotes, and hints on flowers and floral design, these writers express their emotions, with flowers, in a most personal way."

—JIM MORETZ, FOUNDER AND DIRECTOR OF THE AMERICAN FLORAL ART SCHOOL

"Flowers Are Forever *is filled with stories of flower gardens planted, tended, and enjoyed by families, children, neighbors, and communities. It is delightful reading."*

—RUTH STAFFORD PEALE, CHAIRMAN, GUIDEPOSTS INC.

"The beauty and importance of flowers and how they affect our lives is portrayed throughout this heart-warming collection of stories from floral afficionados. Poignant and tender, Flowers Are Forever *will touch the heart. You'll want to read it over and over again. "*

—RICH SALVAGGIO, VICE PRESIDENT OF FLORAL PUBLICATIONS, TELEFLORA, INC.

"A powerful and emotional reminder of the positive influence flowers have had not only in our lives but in the lives of others. Truly inspiring."

—BOB TANEM, AMERICA'S HAPPY GARDENER HOST OF *Tanem in the Garden,* KSFO (SAN FRANCISCO)

"This book reflects moments that are magical and meant to be shared... a perfect gift for those we love."

—PAT VIVO, PROFESSIONAL SPEAKER AND MEMBER OF THE SPEAKERS HALL OF FAME

"A delightful, everlasting bouquet of sentiments and sensibility. This book will be cherished by the flower lover and gardener alike!"

—ROBERT DOLIBOIS, CEO OF THE AMERICAN NURSERY AND LANDSCAPE ASSOCIATION

"The book contains a basic philosophy we at AFS have come to understand, 'We send emotions when we send flowers.' Flowers truly transcend all ethnic and cultural barriers; the gift of flowers needs no translation. This book captures the emotion flowers create in our lives. Just as the fragrance of a flower can transport one back to a place in time, so does this book."

—Tom Butler,
President American Floral Services, Inc. (AFS)

"With today's fast pace, this book has come at an opportune time. The quips of humor, along with the motivational stories, are refreshing. An added bonus are the informative tidbits of floral sense. Flowers have always been my life's inspiration and finding this collection made me stop and smell the roses, again.

—Frank Laning, AAF, AIFD, PFCI,
Floral Coordinator: New York Botanical Garden,
1999 Winter Olympics, Presidential Inaugurations

"The reader will be caught up in how flowers provide a life assuring experience that makes our senses of color (a red carnation), fragrance (lily of the valley), form (dahlia), danger (a roses thorn), taste (nasturtium), and health so rewarding. Your life must include this book of faith in flowers."

—Dr. H. Marc Cathey,
President Emeritus, American Horticultural Society

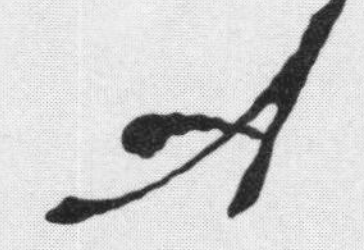

Glorious Garden of More Than 100 Inspirational Stories

A FIRESIDE BOOK

Published by Simon & Schuster

NewYork London Sydney Singapore

Flowers Are Forever

Kathy Lamancusa

FIRESIDE
Rockefeller Center
1230 Avenue of the Americas
New York, NY 10020

DESIGNED BY BARBARA M. BACHMAN

Manufactured in the United States of America
1 3 5 7 9 10 8 6 4 2
Library of Congress Cataloging-in-Publication Data
Lamancusa, Kathy.
Flowers are forever : a glorious garden of more than 100 inspirational
stories / Kathy Lamancusa.
p. cm.
"A Fireside book."
1. Conduct of life. 2. Flowers—Miscellanea. I. Title.
BJ1581.2.L2717 2000
158.1'28—dc21 99-052852
ISBN 0-684-85737-5

DEDICATION

I want to dedicate this book to my sons, Joe and Jim, who taught me that the most precious flowers grow in hidden spots, such as the "Emerald City" of one's own personal woods, and that the beauty of flowers is appreciated around the world, from the crowded streets of Nepal to the wildflowers that grow on the top of Mount Goliath. Thank you for all the flowers you picked and presented to me over the years. I think of them, and you, often while you travel and discover the world.

Wishing

A GLORIOUS GARDEN

OF FLOWERS

TO CELEBRATE LIFE.

Contents

Chapter 4 • Life Lessons

Chapter 5 • To Brighten Our Darkest Hours

ACKNOWLEDGMENTS

Sincere, heartfelt gratitude goes out to every contributor in this book. Each person has looked deeply into their soul, found the special moments in their lives impacted by flowers, and put those moments down on paper to share with others. I could never have imagined when I began this project the full scope and intensity of emotions these stories would elicit.

It was my husband, Joe's, idea to compile the beautiful stories shared with us for our television show, add to them and approach a publisher to bring this work of love to life. I appreciate his unwavering commitment to this project, his laser sharp focus, and his keen insight and guidance to bring it to fruition. His love and support in all aspects of our life and our business permit me to follow the little traveled pathways I can't help but notice and long to discover. Thank you, Joe, for being my life partner!

I want to thank Becky Cabaza, my editor at Simon & Schuster, for her immediate belief in this project and her guidance in making this book a reality. I am also grateful to Peter Miller of the Peter Miller Film & Literary Agency for his excellent job as my agent and manager. His love of this book from the first moment we spoke and his ability to make things happen in the marketplace are incredible assets.

Kay Allenbaugh, best selling author of the *Chocolate for a Woman's Soul* series, supported the concept from the first minute she heard about it, then proceeded to share with me all the advice she worked so hard to get. Thank you, Kay for believing in me and my project, and accepting me as a "Chocolate Sister."

My sister-in-law and business associate, Katherine Lamancusa, provided more than she will ever realize in support, guidance, and assistance throughout all stages of the development of this book. Without her, the process would have been far more difficult. Katherine, you are indispensible!

I first met Ann Lozeau when she was my son Joe's high school English teacher. Through Joe, I heard about some of the most incredible and far reaching life experiences anyone could imagine. She not only inspired Joe through her experiences and stories, she was the single most influential person in his growth and development as a writer. When I needed someone to review this manuscript and be my personal editor, she was the first person who came to mind. She has worked hard with every page and guided me in the fine points of grammar that I didn't even know existed! Thanks, Ann!

A special thanks to Marianne Franko, S. Joseph Lamancusa, Jo Lamancusa, Pat Vivo, and Josie Clarke for their suggestions in the selection process.

Finally, I would like to express my deep appreciation to my maternal grandparents who lived next door as I was growing up and to my father. Although both backyards were small in size, they were filled to overflowing with a glorious abundance of flowers and plants. Many beautiful memories of flowers were planted, grown and cultivated there. Those floral memories remain with me today and prove that flowers are forever.

Introduction

Bread feeds the body indeed, but flowers feed also the soul.

—*The Koran*

Flowers help us celebrate; they inspire our passions, send messages of love and romance, and brighten our days during times of sorrow, illness, and depression. A fresh bouquet is a long-distance hug, a spirit lifter, a stress reliever, providing us with a moment of calm in our hectic lives. Many of life's passages—from birth to death and all the joyous and bittersweet moments in between—are marked by the giving and receiving of flowers. The sight or scent of a particular bloom often causes a flood of emotion-packed memories of a certain time, place, or person. The flowers themselves may not actually last forever, but the memories they evoke most certainly do.

I am honored to have 103 contributors join me in sharing the message of flowers. These contributors are prominent floral designers, influential floral-industry members, motivational speakers, inspirational leaders, creative consultants, therapists, and everyday flower and garden lovers. Through these stories you'll be able to walk in the garden of memories and imagination, and whether you laugh or cry as you travel this path, you'll feel the profound impact that flowers have in our lives.

But there's more. You'll find practical tips to help you enjoy flowers longer and more often. You'll find new ways to incorporate flowers into your life, and you'll learn ways you can use flowers to touch the lives of others.

Flowers have always held a special place in my heart. When I was a child, my grandparents who lived next door were avid gardeners who filled their yard with multitudes of flowers of every size, shape, and color. I spent many an afternoon helping to water, weed, and plant. As I sit here now, I can still see my grandmother with her apron and wide-brimmed hat, her basket over her arm, filled to overflowing with her pickings of the day. The colors and scents will be with me forever.

When my children were growing up, the area behind our house was heavily wooded. There was one special location where a patch of beautiful wildflowers grew each year. Given the name of the "Emerald City" by my sons, this spot became the area that they played in nearly every day. During this time, my office was at home so that I could balance motherhood with a career. I remember one particularly stressful day when I felt I was nearing my wits' end—and in walked Jimmy, my youngest, with his hands behind his back. Never quite knowing what to expect from my free-spirited, enthusiastic son, I braced myself and waited for the inevitable frog, toad, or snake. Instead, he pulled his hands from behind his back and with a huge smile presented me with my very own bouquet of flowers direct from the Emerald City. The day seemed so much better after that!

Having been surrounded by the comfort of flowers throughout my childhood, I turned to flowers as a career. What a joy it has been designing with flowers for books, magazines, newspapers, television, and onstage presentations. I wish I could bring each of you for a visit to the set of our television show. The prep room is always filled to overflowing with flowers that have been shipped in from growers around the world. My guests arrive and spend hours and hours preparing their designs. The days of shooting are long, but everyone involved with our show remains upbeat and happy. I think the reason that the stress doesn't get to them the way it might on a regular television show is that they are surrounded with so many beautiful flowers. I have often seen a camera operator or sound director stop as they walk by and inhale the aroma from a bucket of roses or freesia. Days filled with the breathtaking sights and scents of flowers are like days spent in heaven.

As I speak to audiences around the world, I find that the messages that flowers send are universal messages. The lessons that flowers teach are universal lessons. As you read each of the stories in this book, take a few minutes to embrace its message. Think of this time alone with your thoughts as your own personal journey through the garden of life. You'll find that when you complete your walk, you will be mentally refreshed and deeply moved.

A card my son Joe made for me quoted T. S. Eliot when he said, "We shall not cease from exploration / And the end of all our exploring / Will be to arrive where we started / And know the place for the first time." I hope this book provides you with a garden for exploration and a pathway for your journey. When you finish reading the stories, my wish is that you, too, will find yourself back at the beginning, having become a completely different person through your internal journey of the true messages these inspirational stories have to offer.

But don't stop there. Make flowers a part of your life each and every day. In Europe flowers are considered a necessity, and people will buy flowers to give as a gift or to enjoy themselves several times a week. As flowers carry us through celebration, romance, and sorrow they offer joy and comfort that no words can convey. Whether you prefer an elaborate arrangement of gorgeous blossoms or a simple handful of just-picked flowers from the garden, I think you'll agree that the memories of flowers truly last forever. I'd like to share with you my favorite quote about flowers from James Terry White:

If thou of fortune be bereft,
And in thy store there be but left
Two loaves—sell one, and with the dole
Buy hyacinths to feed thy soul.

Kathy Lamancusa

TO CELEBRATE

I.

MORE THAN ANYTHING,

I MUST HAVE FLOWERS,

ALWAYS, ALWAYS.

—*Claude Monet*

Precious Petals

As the hot August sun beat down on the group of mourners standing around the casket, I couldn't help but feel additional sadness because of all the beautiful flowers that would soon wither and die under the scorching sun. I wanted to capture and retain the warm feeling of love and support that the flowers had provided us with during this difficult time, the loss of my father-in-law.

As I wiped away another tear, a plan quickly began to form in my mind. The funeral director had told us that he had found a birdseed packet in my father-in-law's suit pocket and had carefully tucked it back inside. My father-in-law had watched his first grandchild be married only three weeks earlier, and I remember looking at the other grandchildren surrounding the casket, thinking how sad it would be that he wouldn't be there on their wedding days.

The stately wooden casket was covered with a beautiful funeral spray of crimson-red roses, already beginning to droop in the heat and humidity of the summer day. Several other arrangements contained roses, ready to be placed on the grave. These flowers would quickly shrivel and fade, soon to be discarded by the cemetery personnel. My plan was to gather all the roses from the arrangements, dry the flowers, and use them as the rose petals that the flower girls would sprinkle on the aisle for the grandchildren's wedding days.

My oldest son, Brian, was married recently, and I never

thought on that sad summer day when I started this tradition that my son would have roses from the funerals of three beloved grandparents that would be sprinkled down the aisle. Earlier, he and I had carefully removed the dried roses from their boxes, counted their total, and divided them by the number of grandchildren from each side of the family yet to be married. When we had his share of the roses, we separated the petals one at a time. Through tears of sadness and laughter, we reminisced about his grandparents and how much they would have loved to be sitting in the pew as he and Erin took their vows.

In some small way, as I watched my twin nieces scatter the rose petals on the white runner, I knew that Brian's proud grandparents were smiling from above, providing their love and support, sprinkling their blessings on the radiant couple.

Barb Wingfield

When the life of your fresh roses is almost over, gather all the stems together and hang them upside down in a dry, cool location, allowing the flowers to dry out naturally. The dried flower heads can be glued into designs or decorative accents, or displayed in a lovely crystal bowl or covered jar. Use any discarded dry stems as a design element all their own. Group a few together and use them as a trunk for a topiary tree.

Office Supplies

I have always enjoyed nature and being outdoors, preferably hiking in the woods or strolling through lush landscapes. I wish I could say I find a lot of time to do this, but I don't. Because I work as an office assistant I spend more time surrounded by machines and cement rather than spring breezes and fields of wildflowers, so I have taken it upon myself to bring flowers—roses, sunflowers, and mixed bouquets—each week to set on my desk and brighten my environment. They make me smile.

As I walk into the building, going to my office carrying my weekly armload of flowers, people stop me along the way to comment on the blossoms' loveliness and ask about their recipient. As they approach me, I can't help but notice the way their faces light up, with a big smile slowly appearing. People are always surprised that I buy the flowers for myself!

Clients who come into the office upset and wanting to vent seem to forget for a minute what they are going to yell about when they see the beautiful arrangements on my desk. They crack a smile and say, "What's the occasion?," as they come closer to literally stop and smell the roses. Think about it—ever notice someone delivering flowers to your building? Everyone smiles and approaches the delivery person, hoping that the flowers are for them.

Flowers are a wonderful conversation starter. No one walks away from my desk in a bad mood after seeing my bright, beautiful "office supplies"!

Chandra Wilfong

To be overcome by the fragrance of flowers is a delectable form of defeat.

—*Beverley Nichols*

BOOTLEG BLOSSOMS

"Flowers are essential to our way of life." Amazingly, this statement was made by British prime minister Winston Churchill during a time when my native England was engulfed in war. Road and rail transport had been limited to the movement of troops and munitions. Civilian travel had been reduced to a minimum, mainly by the stringent rationing of gasoline. I remember billboards everywhere that asked "Is your journey really necessary?"

Early in the Second World War, all commercial traffic was banned from passenger trains. This apparently vital restriction effectively and totally cut off London's supplies of spring flowers—daffodils, anemones, violets—from major production areas in the southwest of England, Cornwall, and the Scilly Isles. They were normally shipped from Penzance by rail, and were sold in London's famous Covent Garden flower market.

The ban was a bitter blow to florists in Britain's major metropolitan area. However, before long, black marketeers started bringing in "bootleg" supplies. Their huge suitcases, which they carried as personal baggage, were stuffed full of lovely flowers that were sold in Covent Garden at wickedly inflated prices.

Although we were thankful to have the flowers, regular wholesalers and their customers were outraged at the cost of these normally modestly priced little blooms. A general meeting was convened. Everyone who bought and sold flowers in the market was well represented; even newsmen were called in.

When the story reached the national newspapers, it soon came to the attention of Sir Winston. True to form, he acted swiftly and decisively. He contacted his minister of transport, and the commercial travel ban was immediately lifted.

In the midst of the pressures of war, this prompt and compassionate action effectively saved the livelihoods of Cornish flower producers. It ensured as normal as possible a supply of flowers for the ways of life and death in countless families whose homes and very existences were touched, often ravaged, during those years.

when they decided to up the number. When he left for Desert Storm, they decided to love each other "44." After they were married and moved thousands of miles from family and friends, they increased it to "48." "48" is now their special number, and six years later that is still how much they love each other.

Their fourth anniversary was very special. About 10:00 A.M. there was a knock on her door, and Michelle opened it to the bright smile of a florist holding a dozen red roses. The card read "I love you 12." An hour later came another knock on the door. To my daughter's surprise, there was the florist, again with another dozen red roses. This time the card read, "I love you 24." You guessed it—an hour later there was yet another knock on the door, and yes, another dozen red roses with the card reading "I love you 36." The final arrangement came at 2:00 P.M. It was an exceptionally beautiful vase of red roses sprinkled with baby's breath. The final card read "It has been four wonderful years, enjoy each dozen for each year of marriage—I LOVE YOU 48!"

The combination of loving each other "48" and the beauty of red roses made it a perfect day for my daughter and her husband on their fourth anniversary. Now, not only is 48 a representation of their love for each other, but red roses are also!

Sue Pistone

I go to nature to be soothed and healed,
and to have my senses put in tune once more.

—John Burroughs

My Secret Garden

When my mind travels to places of the heart, flowers always populate my memories.

I recollect, through the eyes of a young child, one breezy, warm spring day. The combination of the sunny day and a crisp blue sky softened by its puffs of cottony clouds resulted in such unforgettable beauty; little crowns of yellow blooms dappled the rich green carpet. I remember their soft touch and woodsy fragrance, their abundance. How lucky I was to have come upon this treasure!

As I recall, I picked the most beautiful of the flowers and was careful not to crush them because, in my childlike imagination, I was creating an offering for the queen. A small princess with a handful of little tufts of sunshine surely would bring a smile.

Just a few gentle years later, my flower world expanded to a magnificent height on another glorious spring day. As I rode my pony through a rolling section of neighboring pastureland, I came upon a large knoll covered with the most breathtaking sight: dainty hedges of lilacs that moved softly with the breeze, in pure harmony, complemented with fragrance.

From the first moment I believed, as only a child could, that this purple hill was my secret place. I returned often to while away the time, dreaming my dreams or imagining faraway places sprinkled with castles and queens, movies and movie stars.

I visited each spring to be awed by its beauty. And each spring the lilacs always bloomed during my birthday month; I felt the blossoms surely were a gift—a joyful gift to lift the heart and delight the spirit of a young girl so many years ago.

Julie Wilkinson

The garden beckons you, come play. Many of us can fondly remember minutes, days, or hours spent in some type of garden in our youth. Some may have memories of a backyard garden filled to overflowing with every color and scent imaginable. Others may remember a walk through the garden in the park that we were able to enjoy only on certain occasions. Some of us may not have had any formal gardens in our lives, but remember the brief glimpses of enjoyment when passing a flower vendor or finding an unexpected flower popping up through the sidewalk. As we move through our busy lives, it is important to follow that child in our mind back to those moments in the garden when heaven met earth. At your most stressful times, close your eyes and come play in the garden. Enjoy the beauty of vivid color, smell the roses, listen to the music in the wind—look, taste, touch, and smell—and relax.

Nature will deliberately reveal itself . . .
if only we look.

—*Thomas Edison*

Mama Lloyd's Orchid

Ever since she fell in love with her Charlie and Hawaii, our dear friend Mama Lloyd had always managed to find an orchid to weave in her long red hair. Her tresses pulled back into a chignon, the orchid would stay nestled against the straight bobby pins. It's easy to find orchids when one lives in the islands, but a move to New York didn't stop the practice. There would be that ever-present orchid—even in the Long Island winters.

They moved to California when Charlie's mind started to wander. His son and daughter-in-law offered support for Mama

Lloyd when Charlie turned cantankerous or did not know who was around. Inevitably, the day came when Charlie's soul waved aloha to this earth. Mama Lloyd was heartbroken. We so wanted to help her, and all we could offer was friendship. And thus she came for dinner—without an orchid.

In our yard we had a pot of orchids whose green-yellow leaves flourished in abundance but never once offered a single blossom. On the night of Mama Lloyd's arrival, I walked out onto the patio. There in its creamy simplicity was a single orchid! We put it in Mama Lloyd's hair. Oddly enough, that plant never bore a blossom again.

Eileen McDargh

What is a weed?
A plant whose virtues have not been discovered.

—*Ralph Waldo Emerson*

Return of the Gardens

My father measures his happiness by the number of things growing around him. Clusters of tulips, shasta daisies, and coralbells. The exotic iris that burst into color in May. Planters spilling over with geraniums and petunias. The new potatoes and vegetables he brings to summer meals.

Years ago he turned the crop fields over to younger men, who rent his farmland, but the flower beds and the vegetable garden are still his domain. My father's perfect day, if he could design it, would include hours of poking things into the dirt, pulling weeds, mowing grass, and coming inside only for a cool drink of water. The day might end by giving a relative or a friend a tour of the grounds. But in the summer of 1994, perfect days were hard to come by.

Earlier in the year, soon after Christmas, my mother complained of a pain in her hip. We assured her that it was probably just the holiday stress. By February, the pain had spread to her thigh, and she often spent her days on the couch. By March, her entire leg burned with pain, and the town doctor was baffled by it. In April, she made an appointment with a specialist in the next town. But he was called away by a family emergency, and the appointment was indefinitely postponed. By May, at a family gathering when we had to help her move from room to room, she was finally desperate enough to listen when I begged her to come and find a specialist in the city where my family and I lived.

We clung to the theory that she had a pinched nerve or a bad back. Our answer came after days of tests. While sitting in a neurologist's office, we learned the word "neuropathy." It refers to severe damage to nerve endings, and in my mother's case it had been brought on by diabetes that had raged out of control. We were told that the pain would subside with medication and proper diet. After a stay in the hospital, Mom returned home. She could barely walk, and her leg muscles were so weak that she began to fall, often in the bathroom, and so she became, essentially, bedridden. My brother, sister, aunt, and I took turns helping at the farm.

But it was my dad who was the day-to-day caregiver. He learned how to test her blood sugar twice a day, give her a complicated round of medications, and prepare special meals for her. When pain overwhelmed her, he rubbed her legs with ointment. I would sometimes hear him talking quietly to her as a sharp, medicinal smell filled the house.

One day in late July, while helping at the farm, I was full of my own complaints and exhaustion. I was helping take care of my mother while also looking after my two little boys and my seven-month-old baby. I walked outside the farmhouse to catch some fresh air. I wandered into the hot garden, hoping to be lifted by the sight of new vegetables and the color of late-summer flowers.

But I could barely make out the garden for the tall weeds. I trampled them down as I walked toward the spot where tomato plants usually grew, then I made my way toward the grapevines and apple trees. It was like stumbling through a forgotten dream. I looked across the land that usually occupied my father in the summer and saw abandonment. His steady, quiet attentions were inside, where he tended his wife of fifty-two years. The garden would wait.

In August, a wonderful thing happened. My mother's pain left her hip and thighs, and the days were more manageable. Her birthday fell on the seventeenth, and she let me read a note Dad had written for her. "I never doubted your recovery," it said. "These past months I have felt closer to you than ever before in our marriage."

Winter came and passed, and the pain slowly lifted. By spring, Mom was doing light housework and cooking meals. She was even doing some gardening in a spot behind a storage shed that she called her "secret garden."

In June, Mom and Dad showed off all the flower beds to their children and grandchildren—blooming hollyhocks, pansies and cosmos, the wrought-iron trellis Dad built for the climbing roses.

The weeds were gone, hacked down by a man happy to be back in his garden. We could look beyond the secret garden and see rows of potatoes. In another direction were the last of the stunning iris, and next to them, the promise of the daylilies, stretching tall, with a look of hope and thankfulness for another growing season.

Toni Wood

A weed can be different things to different people. What is considered a weed in one part of the country could be a prized plant in another. In some cases, weeds are plants that have adapted themselves to survive under the harshest of conditions. Because of this resilience and tenacity, weeds can literally overshadow our gardens if not tended properly. Weeding a garden can be perceived as a chore or as a pleasurable release. Without weeding, carefully planned gardens lose their definition. Gardeners often find weeding a satisfying experience even though it may be tedious. They are saying no to confusion and disorder and yes to clarity and self-reliance. A friend explained that during an extremely trying period of time in her office she took her frustrated rage to the garden and spent time each evening weeding. She said her anger started to subside as she saw its plan reemerge and she was able to think of manageable ways to deal with her situation. Could this simple process of removing that which we don't want so that the beauty of what we do want can become beautifully visible be connected to each of our lives?

ANGELIC CAKE

I was always pleased that my birthday was in May. School was almost out and it was bicycle weather. The kittens were old enough to be playful, and the breeze smelled sweetly of lilac.

My mother traditionally made me an angel food cake—the kind with the sprinkles in the mix—and covered it with white frosting. Year after year its center hole was filled with a small jelly jar holding fresh lily of the valley. To me, this was the most beautiful of birthday cakes!

After I grew up and left home, birthdays were more apt to be beer and bratwurst than cake and ice cream. I had even forgotten about the birthday cake ritual until I had children of my own.

When it was my son's first birthday, I ordered a cake with plain white frosting. At party time, my family teased and joked about the yellow marigolds and bright red geraniums that surrounded Donald Duck on the baby's cake. I guess the memories of the fresh-flower birthday cake had made their way into this new family's traditions.

Though it will never be the spring blossoms of lily of the valley, I doubt if either of my summer-born sons will ever have a cake without fresh flowers on it.

Celeste Lilly-Rossman

For an elegant and simple cake design, cut the stems of flowers short and insert them shallowly into the icing, creating a floral design that lies flat on the cake. The freshness of these flowers can be enhanced with a fine misting of water sprayed on the flowers and leaves before placing them on the cake.

Flower Power

In the '60s, flowers were, to me, a gift of love. Swept up in the idealism of the Aquarian Age, love, peace, and a coming together were very important to me. One of the most beautiful symbols of that time of my life is flowers.

I gave flowers to strangers to encourage thoughts of healing and to symbolize the treasures found in our human relationships. The fragrance of these flowers was a scented, heaven-bound prayer for each person's well-being.

Today, flowers still hold a deep, romantic place in my heart. I love to give and receive them, and their symbolism is still alive for me after all these years. I treasure each person I give flowers to, and the flowers represent that single place where we become as one. Their colors, fragrance, and beauty convey that unity in every bloom.

Eric Larsen

Touch the earth, love the earth, honor the earth,
her plains, her valleys, and her seas;
rest your spirit in her solitary places.

—*Henry Beston*

Daddy's Tree

My husband, Phil, was diagnosed with multiple myeloma, an incurable form of cancer, when our baby, Andrew, was only seven months old. We had moved into our dream house just a few weeks before the diagnosis, at Christmastime, and life seemed very good.

On a sunny winter day, Phil had slipped while shoveling snow and had injured his back. Incredibly, we learned that this very minor accident had broken a vertebra. As devastating as this news was, worse was to come a day or two later when the cancer diagnosis was made. Multiple myeloma often goes undetected until it erodes a bone, and tests confirmed the presence of the always-fatal disease.

Our lives were forever changed. Some pieces of our past remained, but our future became an endless nightmare: tough decisions about treatment, endless days and nights of fear, pain and vigilance, constant worry about money, and tremendous grief and anger. There was so much irony in this new life: Our baby's first steps were paralleled by Phil's careful steps following back surgery. In the hospital, we pushed Phil's wheelchair along next to Andrew's stroller. Our son played with real stethoscopes, borrowed from nurses, when he visited Daddy in the hospital, while other children played with toy doctor kits. Our son's laughter was beautiful to hear, but the flip side was our own tears of grief. Andrew's innocence and trust was in ugly juxtaposition to our loss of innocence and to the wrenching uncertainty invading our lives.

Throughout this time, we struggled to find a silver lining in each day. One of these was my custom of giving Phil a single flower in celebration of completing each round of chemotherapy. As time went on, he received many flowers. Roses, daisies, daffodils, chrysanthemums—beautiful blossoms marking painful milestones.

The flowers were not able to shield us from the fact that the chemotherapy that took so much from Phil was not beating the cancer. Finally, the oncologist ordered an extremely aggressive type of chemo in the hope of getting better results. Knowing that this regimen was going to have even tougher side effects, I decided Phil's homecoming flower this time had to be very special. Since it was December, I went to a garden center nearby and selected a live black spruce tree that was about three feet tall. I decorated it and set it on the hearth of our fireplace, where Phil would see it when I brought him home.

Phil loved the tree, and so did Andrew. Even though he didn't completely understand, I told Andrew that the tree was very special. I said that it was "Daddy's tree," and that our family would plant it outside after Christmas. And so we did. My three older children, all young adults, helped us plant it. Under the direction of their sister, my two tall sons dragged the tree to the backyard, where it suddenly looked much smaller than it had by the fireplace.

I told Andrew we would see how fast both he and Daddy's tree grew. As usual for us, it was a bittersweet occasion. As I snapped a picture of Phil and Andrew by the tree that winter day, I wondered if the tree would survive the winter. And I wondered if Phil would stand beside it again with Andrew the next Christmas.

The years have flown past, and today the tree has grown to a majestic six feet. Andrew is now six years old and still likes to have his picture taken with "Daddy's tree." As I prepare to snap the shot, Phil takes his place next to Andrew. The photo records the child, the tree, and the man, all still growing. My heart records a miracle, a celebration, a gift of God. A "flower" surviving the hard, cold winter of despair, spared against all odds so that it could bloom.

Kathy Baker

If seeds in the black earth can turn into
such beautiful roses, what might not the heart of man
become in its long journey toward the stars?

—*G. K. Chesterton*

Flowers on Parade

In celebration of the arrival of 1889, some of California's newest residents, especially transplanted Easterners who were amazed that flowers bloomed outside in the winter months, gathered blossoms from their yards and the nearby hillsides, decorated their carriages, and began a 110-year-old ritual known today as the Tournament of Roses Parade. The parade has blossomed into the most spectacular and elaborate floral event in the world, with floats that are miracles of engineering, technology, and floral design.

Before a single float ever rolls down Colorado Boulevard in Pasadena, California, on New Year's Day, thousands of people have spent countless hours planning, building, and decorating the moving masterpieces. The final process of covering the massive sculptures with botanicals is a mind-boggling but precisely orchestrated flurry of activity and details.

In early February of every year, after the theme of the next parade is announced, float designers start developing concepts with the corporations that sponsor the flower-encrusted marvels. Every March, after designs are approved, a small army of artists, construction workers, welders, and hydraulic engineers, working from sketches, blueprints, and small models of each float, starts to bring the designers' concepts to life. Nine months later, construction is finished, and the resulting "sculptures," which are built of steel rods and covered in aluminum screen, are ready to be covered in fresh flowers.

During the decorating phase, flowers and other botanicals are either poked through the aluminum-screen skin of the floats or are glued on with one of seven specially formulated glues. Float builders primarily use volunteers during this phase—generally, individuals or organizations such as high school bands and choirs or church youth groups. It is also common for employees of float-sponsoring companies to volunteer to work on their particular company's float.

Jim Hynd Jr., AIFD, a floral designer, one of the founders of the American Institute of Floral Designers, and a co-owner of Fiesta Parade Floats, the second-largest builder of rose parade floats in the country, explains, "During decorating week, which runs from December twenty-sixth through the thirtieth, an average crew ranges in size from fifty to one hundred people per shift, and we run two eight-hour shifts a day. Larger floats have even larger crews—up to three hundred people."

For floats sponsored by FTD, Inc., the floral wire-service organization that has had entries in every rose parade for the last forty-four years, a dozen or so florists are hired and another two hundred volunteers are used. In one year, FTD's float decorators can work a total of about thirteen thousand hours during the five days before the parade.

Every year, Mr. Hynd receives inquiries from scores of florists across the country who want to work on a float. He is quick to caution them that float decorating is not glamorous—it's cold, wet, dirty, and tiring—and that they are expected to work whatever hours it takes to complete the floats on time.

"I prepare a schedule for each float with what's necessary to be done every day. If any of the crews run behind during decorating week, they are required to stay until the work scheduled for that day is finished. Sometimes crews will have to stay until two or three o'clock in the morning. The last night, December thirtieth, is always all night, because the judging of the floats starts on the morning of the thirty-first, the day before the parade."

For the most part, fresh flowers and foliage for rose parade floats are purchased from the same commercial flower growers who supply traditional retail and wholesale florists. And even though float companies buy enormous quantities of flowers—often entire fields—they still pay market prices. Mr. Hynd states that today about 60 percent of the over 20 million blooms used in the Rose Parade are grown in California, but tropicals may come from Hawaii; carnations, roses, and pompons may come from Colombia and Ecuador; dendrobium orchids may come from Thailand; and other flowers are imported from Holland.

In addition to the decorating crews, other crews are assembled for receiving, processing, and distributing the flowers as well as for filling and capping the water tubes. The processing crew cuts all flowers under water and puts them in preservative solution in freshly scrubbed buckets. All of the roses are dipped in citric acid, and bud openers are used for carnations and lilies. The flowers are processed for use the same way most florists prepare elements of individual arrangements.

In one year, Fiesta Parade Floats' processing crew can handle 152,000 bunches of pompons, 36,000 bunches of carnations, and over 20,000 bunches of roses. During processing, the crew puts approximately 150 roses or 200 to 250 carnations in each bucket. That means over 7,200 buckets for roses and carnations alone.

Another crew manually fills and caps over one million water tubes and puts them on sheets of foam. "They can fill and cap over fifteen thousand tubes in an hour," Mr. Hynd relates. "Then, flowers such as roses, irises, gerbera daisies, and carnations are cut to about eight inches in length, put in the vials, labeled for their appropriate float, and stored in four refrigerated semitrailers." Preservative is not used in the water tubes because they're filled so far in advance that by the time flowers are put in them, the preservative has lost its strength.

So that these floral wonders, when finished, can be maneuvered through the areas required to get them to Pasadena, size restrictions are imposed. Floats can not exceed fifty-five feet in length, eighteen feet in width, or seventeen feet in height. "However," Mr. Hynd notes, "with the use of hydraulics and the complex mechanics of today, floats can expand to greater dimensions as long as they can retract to comply with the size restrictions." Hydraulics give today's float designers almost unlimited creative opportunities, and depending on the complexity, they can push the price of a float to over a quarter of a million dollars.

Certainly those Californians who decorated their carriages with flowers in 1889 could never have imagined that their efforts would inspire such a spectacular event that would be viewed by millions of people around the world each January.

David L. Coake

HEARTS AND FLOWERS

2.

RISE UP, MY LOVE,
MY FAIR ONE, AND COME AWAY.
FOR, LO, THE WINTER IS PAST,
THE RAIN IS OVER AND GONE.
THE FLOWERS APPEAR
ON THE EARTH;
THE TIME OF THE SINGING
OF BIRDS IS COME,
AND THE VOICE OF THE TURTLE
IS HEARD IN OUR LAND.

—Song of Solomon 2:10–12

The Black Rose

They were in love. The two high school sweethearts had been together since the ninth grade. Both also shared a love for beautiful flowers. It seemed as if flowers were their main topic of conversation, except when they were expressing their adoration for each other.

In January 1965, during his senior year, young John turned eighteen. As was required of all young men, he registered for the draft, fulfilling his duty but feeling a sense of impending uneasiness. Then, the feeling was realized. On June fifteenth, the inevitable happened. Young John received greetings and salutations from Uncle Sam; he had been drafted.

Feeling mixed emotions, the young couple discussed the impact of the draft notice on their relationship and reached a decision. They decided that they would marry immediately. On June twentieth they were married, and on July first young John was off to basic training.

The young bride wrote to her new husband every day, pages and pages of how much she missed him, and how wonderfully alive the fall flowers and colors were.

Young John finished his basic and advanced training. But, the young newlyweds' world crashed—he received orders for Viet Nam.

It was then that the young bride made a promise to her husband. Each month while he was away, she would send him a different flower and the reason for having chosen that particular flower for him. Their hearts were aching as young John shipped out, for it was indeed a sad day for them.

The young bride was true to her word. The first month she sent a pressed white rose to tell him she would be faithful, a sign of true love for him. Another month she sent him a yellow rose to signify how he brightened her life.

When the young soldier was in his tenth month of duty, his wife sent him a black rose, along with the alarming words, "I sent the black rose because I fear for your life. I have been having horrible dreams." She begged him to be careful.

As was his habit, the young soldier placed the flower from his wife in his left breast pocket, over his heart, but this time he also placed his well-worn Bible in that pocket.

Later that day in an ambush, the young soldier was struck in the chest with an AK-47 round and knocked unconscious. He awoke in the field hospital, his chest covered with a small bandage. On a tray beside him lay the black rose and the Bible, each with a small hole through them. The power of love? Definitely. The strength flowers give us? Undoubtedly. And the wonderful grace of God? Most assuredly!

John and his bride of thirty-three years are schoolteachers nearing retirement. They own and operate a greenhouse, creating wonderful colors with their flowers. They are working on developing the perfect black rose.

Allen D. Walters

Roses lose moisture through cells that are located under the leaves or on the stem. After cutting a rose, remove the lower third of the leaves on the stem; you will reduce the amount of evaporation the flower will undergo, which will lead to a longer life for it.

Flowers are the sweetest things that God ever made
and forgot to put a soul into.

—Henry Ward Beecher

The Heirloom Rose

A business acquaintance had asked me to meet him for drinks. Reluctantly, I accepted the invitation. Well, I fell in love in one short evening. Of course, I had no idea where his thoughts were.

The next day I was flying to Dallas for a business trip. He offered to take me to the airport. A good sign! I felt my affections might be reciprocated.

Every day of my business trip, I returned to my room to find one long-stemmed rose. My new beau, Dennis, colluded with Sylvia, the hotel's receptionist, to carry out his wishes. The first night there was a red rose, then a white rose, and then a yellow rose. I, in turn, learned of Sylvia and made a point of thanking her for her efforts on both of our behalfs.

Three days later, with luggage, purse, briefcase, and airline ticket, I was finally going home. I had a vase of flowers that were still fresh and pretty. I chose to carefully wrap them for Sylvia to enjoy. When I approached her, she would not hear of my leaving the flowers behind but instead created an aluminum-foil traveling vase for my roses. So off to the airport I went, luggage, purse, briefcase, airline ticket, and roses!

Dennis was waiting for me at the airport, as eager to see me as I him. He was amazed that the roses had made the trip. Once back to my place, out of politeness he took a deep breath to inhale their fragrance. Immediately he started a sneezing jag that literally ended the evening abruptly (although quite humorously). I never got the flowers in a vase and just left them on the kitchen counter.

Our courtship was short-lived because we chose to be married four months after that Dallas trip. Our daughter was born before our first wedding anniversary.

The first rose, the red one, dried beautifully, intact. I had it mounted in a two-inch-deep shadow-box frame that hangs in our bedroom today. I intend to pass it on to our daughter with all the love, affection, and adoration it represents. I'm sure that by the time she is old enough to enjoy the story, she will have already learned firsthand from her father what true devotion and affection are all about.

Pat Klima

Arranging a dozen roses can be done quickly and easily. Insert several stems of leatherleaf fern in a rose vase. Gather all the rose heads together and cut the stems to the same length. Insert them in the vase and all the roses will fall into place. Add an accent of ribbon or raffia tied around the neck of the vase.

Lulu and Brigadier

At our London flower shop, we became quite used to a regular telephone call for a small posy of flowers to be sent to "Lulu, c/o Mrs. Button" with a little card saying "Love from Brigadier." It sounded romantic, and we tried to imagine Lulu as well as her tall, handsome brigadier. When the flowers were delivered, an elderly lady always took them, so we continued to wonder what Lulu was like. Afterward, we would get a call from Mrs. Button to send flowers to Brigadier "c/o Lady Chapell" with the card "Would you like to come for tea? Love from Lulu." This went on for some time. Both Mrs. Button and Lady Chapell had regular accounts with us, but we were intrigued by what we thought was a romance.

One day her ladyship arrived at the shop in a beautiful Rolls-Royce. A very charming, dear old lady, she stated, "I have Brigadier with me." This sounded very interesting, and when we asked, "Would he like to come into the shop?" She said, "No, he can stay in the car." As she was leaving, we were all eager to see the brigadier. He sat on a rug on the backseat, a very handsome, well-spotted Dalmatian. We found out that the girlfriend, Lulu, was a French poodle. The exchange of flowers was the two ladies' idea of sending flowers to each other as a friendly gesture when it was not a special occasion.

Kathleen Bretherick

Gently steed our spirits, carrying with
them dreams of flowers.

— William Wordsworth

Sweetheart Roses

Several years ago, I traveled from New Jersey to be a bridesmaid in my girlfriend's wedding in Ohio. At the reception, I met a nice gentleman, enjoyed his company, and had a wonderful time. I really didn't think anything would come of that evening since he lived in Ohio and I was going home the next day.

A few days later, back at work, I got three beautiful white roses from the gentleman in Ohio. I was caught totally off guard and was very pleased. The bride and groom were off on their honeymoon, so I'm not really sure how he found me other than from my having mentioned where I worked during our conversation.

I had to get his phone number from the operator because we hadn't exchanged numbers; but I did call him to thank him, and our relationship began. As it turned out, he was going to be in New Jersey in two weeks and he wanted me to meet him. I did, and we had a great time.

Later that week, I received three more white roses. A few weeks later, I met him in New York; he was going to be there on business. We went to three plays and had dinner and another lovely time. Again, a few days later, I received more white roses. The phone conversations continued and so did the roses. We were dating across four hundred miles; every Friday that I was not going to see him, he would send three white sweetheart roses.

Now the funny thing about this was, I wasn't really sure where this relationship would end up, but I knew I would feel awfully guilty if I dated anyone after getting the roses. So did he. I think it was his master plan to get me to fall in love with him. When I visited him in Ohio, he would have white sweetheart roses in every room of the house.

Early in our courtship, he asked me to marry him; but I had had my heart broken in a previous marriage that had ended in divorce and was in no hurry to be married again. He never got discouraged, he just sent more roses. Several months later, he asked me to marry him a second time; again, I turned him down because the next guy I married was going to have to walk on water. Nevertheless, he sent more roses.

After almost a year of dating, he proposed again. For the third time I said no, and still I got flowers. It dawned on me that even though he couldn't walk on water, this guy was terrific! He truly cared about me, and I believed that he loved me as much as I loved him. So I wrote him a letter saying, "If you are still asking, the answer is yes." Guess what? I got a dozen long-stemmed red roses with a card that read "In response to the answer of yes, the question is, 'Will you marry me?' "

We have been happily married for over sixteen years. I still get white sweetheart roses from him on special occasions, but, better yet, I get them for no reason at all!

Kathy G. Wise

The messages flowers send continue to be expressed long after the flowers move from their fresh state into a dried afterlife. Sharon Oxley's husband has given her one red rose on every birthday and Christmas for the past sixteen years. She saves each one, and after it is dried, she places the petals in a special jar on her windowsill, continually scenting them with rose oil. Since her husband is a salesman and travels each week, she often finds herself home alone. She knows the flame still burns strongly each time she passes the jar and is reminded of his love. Why not take the next flowers you receive and dry them by hanging them upside down or laying them flat with space between each flower? Leave them in a warm, dark place till they are dry to the touch. The dried heads can then be removed and showcased in a special container for all to see.

There is a garden in every childhood,
an enchanted place
where colors are brighter, the air softer, and
the morning more fragrant than ever again.

—*Elizabeth Lawrence*

My Lifeguard

Bill and I met when we were sixteen-year-old lifeguards at the local Y. He was my first, true love. My heart broke when we finally got together after college, only to be separated once again when I got a job at a New York City newspaper's Albany bureau three hundred miles away.

Life went on. I missed him terribly but poured myself into my work. Four years later we ran into each other in the parking lot of New Jersey's Meadowlands Arena, where we had both gone to watch our siblings graduate from Montclair State University. Out of thousands of parking spots, the people we were with had parked in the same row. We chatted for only a moment. It was raining, and Bill was walking with a tall blond. If looks could have killed, I would have been dead.

I was in a fog that night and the next day at work. At lunch, to get my mind off Bill, I decided that I would take a quick walk and bring back something delicious. On my way out of the building, I passed a flower delivery person carrying two dozen gorgeous red and white roses. I love flowers and thought to myself, "Someone's very lucky. I wish it were me." Determined to change my mood, I continued on my quest for the perfect lunch. When I returned, the office was in a buzz. As I entered my office, the overwhelming bouquet was on my desk. Its card read: "You look beautiful in the rain." Bill had tracked me down, and with his gift of flowers, had wiped away years of heartbreak.

A little more than two years later, we were married. You can guess what the flowers were at the wedding: all roses, on everything from the hand-painted invitations, to the centerpieces, to the cake.

I dried the flowers, keep some in a decorative container in our kitchen, and have tucked a few away in my journal to show our grandchildren. When readying for my move into our condo,

I came across an old journal. A dried white rose, a gift from Bill, tumbled out. I remember that rose, once fresh; but it was still beautiful, and I know our love has come full circle and into full bloom.

Lonni Miller Ryan

Use homemade rosewater as a soothing and refreshing facial rinse and as an after-bath splash. Place 1 1/2 cups bottled spring water, 1/8 cup 100-proof vodka, and 1 1/2 cups fresh, fragrant, organically grown rose petals of any color into a clean 1-quart glass jar. Cover and shake. Store in the refrigerator for one week, shaking daily. Strain out the rose petals and either pour the rosewater into an atomizer or apply with a cotton ball. It can be stored in the refrigerator for up to two weeks.

There is a true music of Nature; the song of the birds,
the whisper of leaves, the ripple of waters upon
a sandy shore, and the wail of wind or sea.

—*John Lubbock*

Friday Flowers

When I was twenty, I worked as a buyer for a department store in Texas. One day a salesman from Illinois called and when my boss introduced me as the buyer, I could tell from the look on the salesman's face that he'd expected someone considerably older. Erwin was selling Christmas lights, novelties, and a line of electric percolators, but he made it clear that he'd also like a date. I wasn't interested in this total stranger. For all I knew, he could be married and have a bevy of little ones, so I summoned up all my professionalism and made my position quite clear.

The next morning, a lovely corsage arrived at the office. It was from Erwin. The following day, another arrived, and on Friday a big bouquet of fresh flowers was waiting for me at home. Erwin had mentioned to my boss that he'd like to take me out, but my boss had told him that he probably didn't have much of a chance. I guess Erwin felt he needed to do something extra to get my attention.

Then letters began arriving—several each week—but I tossed them out unopened. Unbeknownst to me, and so I wouldn't miss out on a "good thing," my boss's wife, Georgia, and her sister, Henrietta (both of whom worked at the store), had taken it upon themselves to begin writing to Erwin in my name.

Corsages continued to arrive at the office, as did bouquets at home on the weekends. At first I was annoyed, but later intrigued by his persistent, unacknowledged attentions.

Finally I read one of his letters and was dismayed to find "we" had been corresponding. Georgia and Henrietta confessed their matchmaking endeavors. I wrote an apology, but also found his responses interesting and sensitive.

For more than two years I received both corsages and bouquets. Over time we fell in love and married. There have been many flowers over our fifty years, and five children as well.

It's probably not remarkable that together we built a business that provides supplies to the floral industry.

Louise G. Weder

Flowers have a language all their own. Send a message with the flowers you select:

Pink carnation—"I'll never forget you."
Gardenia—"You're lovely."

Orchid—"You're beautiful."
Red tulip—"My perfect lover."
Ivy—"I'll never betray you."
Chrysanthemum—"May you have a long life."

Love is a tender plant; when properly nourished,
it becomes sturdy and enduring, but neglected
it will soon wither and die.

—*Hugh B. Brown*

Musical Roses

There are two elements in my life that have become intimately connected: roses and music. Roses bring back memories of times spent chatting with my grandmother. I recall that most of our conversations took place while Gram washed dishes and I sat next to her on a wooden stool that she had painted especially for me. She was someone very special, and she reminded me of roses, those delicate, sweet flowers that radiate love. Music also brings back memories of joyous times together with friends and family, as well as the times I use it to relax and renew.

After marrying, I shared my love of roses with my husband, and he responded by often bringing them home to me. Suddenly, however, he stopped. For months I said nothing, trying to convince myself that they were not important because I had so many blessings. Why should I worry about roses? But their absence got the better of me, so I finally asked him, "Why don't you bring roses anymore?"

Looking directly at me he calmly stated, "I just hate to see them die."

On our next anniversary, and not so surprisingly, I again received roses. But this time their beauty was preserved forever, enclosed in a crystal case as part of a music box. What a lovely sight and sound.

This past anniversary he repeated his gift. The roses are different, as is their song, but I'm thinking now that I'd better find some space for all the roses to come that will last forever.

Gram has moved on to a special place, yet I know that she is looking down and showering her love on each and every fragile rose that blooms—and passes.

Euneata Payne

Lilacs remind me of my grandmother. She had a huge wall of them all along the back of her yard. The fragrance was as memorable as the flowers were beautiful. When I was a child, I used to pick a blossom and tuck it into my book bag or, when I was older, my car. At the end of the day, even after the flower had wilted, the aroma was still wonderful. Today, every time I smell lilacs, I think of my grandmother. What floral scents bring back wonderful memories for you?

Open the door; let in the air,
The winds are sweet and
the flowers are fair.
Joy is abroad in the world today.

—*British Weekly*

Worth Every Penny

I grew up in a small village in the Danish countryside, never thinking of flowers as a commercial product since they were always free for the picking—in the fields, the forests, the gardens, and along the roadside.

As a small boy, I picked big bouquets for my mother, especially for Mother's Day. When I grew a little older and got my "bike license," I rode to a nearby nursery where for years I got, for free, a gloxinia for Mother's Day from the nice nursery lady who apparently liked me. I did not know flowers had a price.

Grown up, gone to the city to meet fame and fortune, and now armed with a proper driver's license and a borrowed car, I stopped at a florist to send my mother a proper Mother's Day arrangement for the very first time. The florist, a young, tall, blonde beauty, caught my interest, but she was busy, and an attempt to chat her up a little took some time, beyond the actual ordering of the flowers. By now it was 4:00 P.M., rush hour, and the "strictly no parking" rules were always enforced in this area. 4:15 P.M.! Then 4:30! The parking fine was three times the price of the flowers. It was an expensive conversation, but well worth the cost. I married the florist eighteen months later. That was thirty years ago.

And as for my mother, she enjoyed *those* flowers very much!

Poul Einshøj

The butterfly counts
not months but moments and
has time enough.

—*Rabindranath Tagore*

The Wooing

Most of the time when customers come into our shop they're unsure of what they want, and so we have to pull their desires out of them. These are the ones who want "just something" for a special occasion. But, sometimes, people know precisely the effect they are trying to create.

One day one of these rare people came into my flower shop. He was a very ordinary-looking person, neither handsome nor ugly, with a comfortable Saturday look, slightly rumpled, only a faint growth of beard. I let him get the feel of the flowers and the styles we had to offer and when I judged he was ready, I approached him.

I discovered that this man had very specific needs. He wanted a big, luxurious, romantic bouquet to be sent to an inn two weeks hence. He knew he wanted some roses; he liked the stargazer lilies, a lot; he wanted the freesias for their fragrance. And he wanted them all in a basket that would be worth keeping. This man really knew what he was after and I inquired if this might be for a honeymoon or an anniversary. He replied, "Well, not exactly. This is for a wooing!"

A wooing! I'd never met someone actually planning a wooing. While it's the sort of thing you might read of, most people aren't even comfortable with the word!

This was a special wooing. He and his girlfriend had been separated by a business move and had carried on their courtship with half the continent between them. With the upcoming event he was planning to "pop the question."

He also purchased not one or two, but five gardenias to float in the Jacuzzi and a box of rose petals to strew over the bed linens and bath.

Perhaps, when a man wants to impress a woman, wooings should become more popular. How could anyone say no after experiencing this incredibly romantic evening!

Alison E. Webb

When celebrating a special anniversary, Carol Scherm suggests that you include a request for a single flower in place of a gift. She did just that on her twenty-fifth wedding anniversary and received fifty-seven beautiful roses!

When using a clear glass container, fill it with stones, marbles, iridescent cellophane, or charcoal to provide a foundation that will conceal floral foam.

The Double Daisy

My daughter, Leslie, has always loved gerbera daisies and wanted to have them in her wedding bouquet. But when we spoke with the florist, we were told that the gerberas might not "hold up" in the bouquet. Disappointed, Leslie decided to use another flower.

The afternoon before the wedding, I went to a friend's house to have my hair done. As she worked, she told me about her beautiful garden and the gerbera daisies that she grew. Then she told me that she had a prized gerbera that had somehow produced two beautiful flowers on one stem. My friend had no idea how much Leslie loved gerbera daisies nor how sad she had been that she couldn't use them in her bouquet. When I told my friend, she led me to her garden to show me her magnificent flowers. As she cut the double daisy and handed it to me, she said, "This is God's way of saying that this marriage will be a beautiful union; Leslie must have it." When I got home I handed the flower to a joyful, astonished Leslie.

Priscilla Hauser

The gerbera is also known as the African daisy and the Barberton daisy. The use of floral preservatives can nearly double its vase life. Gerberas are very susceptible to bacterial blockage and blockage at the water line. Any dirt or bacterial formation can clog the vascular system and collapse the flower. Always place them in clean, clear water that is not too deep. Recut the stems before placing in water. One of the problems with gerberas is that in some varieties the stems are prone to weakness. This can easily be assisted by floral-taping a twenty-gauge length of wire with the lighter green floral tape. Then form the top into a bend or hook shape that will rest just under the head of the flower. Floral-tape the rest of the wire to the stem of the flower.

Grandpa's Prom Flowers

My family had been a part of the community for many years and became more so with the opening of our flower shop on the city's square. Generations of families had lived in this small town and flourished. Many of the town's children had returned to it to take up their parents' professions as doctors, lawyers, teachers, and shopkeepers. Such was the case with the local family of dentists.

As prom time approached, the daughter of the middle-aged dentist ordered her flowers from us, but we, accidentally, posted them to the wrong account.

When the senior version of the dentist came into our store to inquire about the bill he had received, we noted our error and explained the flowers. To our surprise, he responded, "You have no idea how *delighted* I would be to pay for my granddaughter's prom flowers."

Our posting error gave great satisfaction to a grandfather who was only too eager to pay, and we often wondered if we should make more mistakes by "including" grandparents in such special occasions.

Alan K. Parkhurst

Our Nameless Rose

As we drove up to the little church, we noticed that the lights were dim and that there weren't any other cars out front. I turned to my friend Valerie and said, "Are you sure this is the place?" She read the address on the crumpled slip of paper she pulled from her pocket. "Yes, we're where we should be." We tried the doors and they were locked. We knocked several times and got no answer.

"I don't understand this," said Valerie, "this *is* the third Sunday, and they're supposed to be having a service here tonight." As I peered through the locked doors searching for a sign of life, I was wondering what I'd gotten myself into. I hadn't been attending church regularly at that point in my life.

Before I could utter a sigh of relief for not having to sit through who knows what, Valerie tugged my arm. "Look! Look! Over there!" She was pointing across the parking lot to a large three-story office building. "Could *that* be it? Let's go see." I mumbled to myself as we strode across the parking lot. The building was well lit, and cars were lining up, yet I couldn't quite accept that a church could be there, in a big, ugly, office building. I looked above and read the sign—EMMANUEL HOUSE OF PRAYER.

This certainly didn't look anything like the churches I'd attended. No stained glass. No big crosses to mark the main entrance. No marble bowls filled with holy water. Just carpet, more doors, and a staircase.

As we were hesitating, we were met by an elegant older lady with shiny silver-and-black hair. On the lapel of her overcoat was a giant red cabbage rose. Valerie nudged me as she noticed it, too.

"Don't be afraid to come in," the lady said softly. "Everybody's welcome in our congregation. We just moved into this building. Tonight is the first service here."

We followed the "rose lady," as Val and I now call her, to the top of the stairs. We sat down in the back amid rows of mismatched folding chairs just as the service was beginning. Valerie leaned over and whispered, "What did you think of that big rose? Neat, huh? Didn't you tell me one time about some saint who likes roses?"

"Uh-huh. That's Saint Theresa. She sends roses when prayers are answered."

"Well, I hope you're right, because you know we need them."

Valerie and I had decided to attend the prayer service to ask God's blessing since, at the time, we were both working full-time as nurses in a hospital, raising our families, and coping with our own chronic health problems. Working at the hospital had become a struggle. We wondered if we really made a difference in our patients' lives. Did our knowledge amount to anything? Were we "angels of mercy," or were we just a couple of warm bodies who got the work done?

I listened intently as each member of the congregation stepped up to the microphone to share his woe, and how God had come to the rescue. Their stories of faith and courage caused a swelling of emotion, and feelings of tenderness—ones that hospital burnout had nearly erased. Only when Valerie handed me her hankie did I realize just how much I'd been crying. As I looked around the room, I saw men and women—young and old, black and white—all equally moved.

The pastor called up the last congregation member to give

her story. She walked slowly and deliberately toward the microphone. Her trembling hands gripped the microphone as she choked back tears. It was the rose lady. Through quivering lips, she spoke. "I wanted to say just how happy God had made me, but I just can't do that right now. I don't know what's happening to me. I just want everyone here to pray for me. *Please!* I can't drive anymore, I fall asleep. I even had an accident, I'm just so tired all the time. I don't know why, but I'm so, so tired." She hung her head, as if in shame, and handed the microphone to the pastor's wife without even looking up.

Stunned, Valerie and I just stared at each other. We jumped from our seats and headed for the doorway. We needed to catch the rose lady. "Excuse me, ma'am," I said, "but we need to talk to you."

"Yes, ma'am," Valerie interjected, "we're nurses, and we know that you have a real medical problem."

"That's right," I added. "We know because we both have the same problem that you do."

"I have sleep apnea," Valerie said.

"Do you know about narcolepsy?" I asked. "These are sleep disorders, and there are doctors for this. You can get treated—we go to a doctor right here in town. Would you like his name?"

The rose lady's face brightened. She smiled and nodded yes. As I reached into my purse to find a pen to write down the doctor's name, I found, instead, an old appointment card of his tucked inside the frayed lining of my purse. I handed the worn, folded card to the rose lady. She held it to her chest and leaned forward to hug us. Tears in her eyes, she looked heavenward and exclaimed, "Thank you!" After hugging me, she let go, adjusted her lapel, fluffed the big rose, snuffed a big sniffle, and walked out the door.

Although we never did learn her name, or get a prognosis on her problem, we did regain our faith in ourselves and in nursing.

We haven't been back to that church, but we did learn that the little church across the parking lot, the one we were originally headed for, had its own congregation and that they did hold special services every third Sunday. The evening of our visit, oddly enough, turned out to be the fourth Sunday.

Terri Quillen

THE GIFT OF FLOWERS

3.

SPRING UNLOCKS
THE FLOWERS TO PAINT
THE LAUGHING SOIL.

—*Reginald Hever*

A Flower for the Gentleman

When I was about six or seven, I remember getting dressed up to go visiting friends with my parents. In those days, I think every Catholic boy had a navy blue suit to wear for mass and visiting. I felt very grown up when I put that suit on. As we were leaving the hostess's home, it started to pour. Since we didn't have a car, we huddled under umbrellas and started walking home. Just as we'd set out, a car came by and splashed me. I felt as terrible as terrible could be. From her front door, my parents' friend, Madge, saw what happened and asked us back inside. Sensing my disappointment, she assured me that the suit could be dried and cleaned and would be as good as new. She also said, "How could a fine gentleman like you not have a flower in his lapel?" I didn't even know what a lapel was!

She broke off a piece of honeysuckle from a vine near her front door and inserted the flower in my lapel. The beautiful smell was matched by her thoughtfulness. It was still pouring, but my heart was full of sunshine. Madge died many years ago, but I always think of her when I see honeysuckle—and I have a lot growing in my yard. In her honor, I wear a flower in my lapel as often as the occasion allows.

Tony DeMasi

The Power of a Single Flower

After teaching an all-day class in basic floral design to over a hundred students, we had accumulated as many fresh flower arrangements as there were students. We decided to contact a local assisted-living facility to see if they would accept the flowers. They were overjoyed and the arrangements were loaded for delivery.

We were greeted at the front entrance of the facility by the director, who instructed us to place the designs in the recreation room for distribution throughout the home later in the evening. As we carried the flowers into the facility, an elderly lady, a tattered shawl covering her frail shoulders, was slumped in her wheelchair, head drooping, appearing despondent, weak, and frail, but as each of us walked by her, she would raise her eyes and gaze at every arrangement that passed.

On my last trip to the recreation room, I removed a single yellow daisy pompon. Approaching her, I knelt holding this brilliantly colored flower to her eyes, asking, "Would you like to have this?" Without speaking a word, my new friend gently reached out from under her shawl, head still down, and took the beautiful blossom into her hand.

As I returned to the van parked at the front door, I looked back to see this wonderful lady holding the daisy to her eyes with a smile so radiant that it matched the color of the flower. In that moment I was reminded that the simple gesture of offering someone even a single flower can bring immeasurable joy.

Richard L. Milteer

Water is essential in the floral conditioning process to extend the life of a flower. The moment you bring your flowers into the house, put them in the deepest container of water, with preservative solution, for as long as possible. Several hours for purchased flowers or overnight for garden blooms is recommended. Use tepid or warm water, which the stems will absorb more quickly than cold water. Place the container in a cool spot that is free of drafts and let them take a good, long drink before you arrange them.

They will come and shout for joy, they will rejoice in the bounty of the Lord—They will be like a well-watered garden, and they will sorrow no more.

—Jeremiah 31:12

FRIENDS ARE FLOWERS THAT NEVER FADE

Emotions rushed through my body while thoughts raced through my mind. I lay flat on my back on the wheeled stretcher looking up at the moving ceiling, wondering about my future. Ambulance drivers were wheeling me down the long corridor to my new room at the Dodd Hall Rehabilitation Center on the campus of The Ohio State University, where I taught.

It had been five days since my accident. While riding my bicycle, an eighty-foot tree had fallen and crushed me. My spinal cord was damaged and my back and neck were broken. I was paralyzed from the waist down. Scared beyond belief and absorbed by agonizing thoughts, I was uncertain of the extent of my injuries and fearful of the rehabilitation process I was facing.

We all know that bad news travels fast. My story made the TV news and the local paper. The story also spread via word of mouth and E-mails among friends, colleagues, and even the professional speakers' association I belonged to.

The flowers and potted plants started arriving the day I did. When I spotted the first arrangement, I was both excited and curious to read the attached card. The deliveries continued, seemingly nonstop. I was surprised that so many friends, relatives, colleagues, students, clients, and neighbors cared so much for me.

After a few days, visitors began arriving, many bringing flowers. Every time I left the room for therapy, more flowers appeared. It became a memory exercise to determine where the new floral pieces had been placed. I tried to remember who gave me each piece, but was soon exhausted by this practice.

Soon I was running out of room for the arrangements. Window ledges, both nightstands, even the bathroom was full! Doctors and nurses who came to my room to treat me stopped at the door in amazement. They had never treated a patient in a flower shop.

The sweet scents of roses, carnations, and freesias masked the harsh smell of hospital disinfectants and brought many curious staff members to visit.

With the sun shining on the flowers and plants, my room looked like an indoor garden, and I was astounded by the outpouring of love from so many. I realized how extraordinarily lucky I was to still be alive and to be able to enjoy my life with those people who had sent me so much.

At night, however, only shadows were visible, and time for me was very difficult. I wore a very uncomfortable neck brace twenty-four hours a day, my sternum was fractured, and the pressure from the neck brace touching my chest caused me pain. My back hurt, my hip hurt, my chest hurt. I couldn't turn my body or regulate my body temperature. Sleep was nearly impossible. I lay alone, in pain, with thoughts of what body functions I had lost. Tears streamed down my cheeks.

Trying to force my thoughts to anything that was pleasant, I could see the silhouettes of the floral arrangements in my darkened room. Night lights by the floor as well as lights from the parking lot provided just enough visibility. One helium balloon, attached to a dozen roses, slowly swayed in the night. Its movement gave me something to focus on. Its message, "Get Well Soon," was both touching and motivational.

As the daylight came, I decided to give away my gifts. I instructed a nurse to take some to the nurses' station. I gave some to my mother, who kept some and gave others away to her ailing neighbors. I told two therapists to take some home to their spouses. I felt much better giving these flowers to others to enjoy. My thoughts turned to helping others and away from my pain and fears.

As the flowers began to fade, they had to be discarded. The friends, however, who bloomed in the days, weeks, and months after returning home will never fade, but will continually bring me gardens of love.

Rosemarie Rossetti

Several years ago when I was speaking in England, my husband and I took our two sons along in an effort to turn this trip into a working vacation. We had an exciting nine-day vacation, then the boys were to go back to the States and my husband, Joe, and I were going to stay behind for the presentation I was to give. Joe accompanied the boys to the airport in the service of a British driver. On their way there, they were in a serious car accident. The first few days and weeks were very traumatic, and since we were overseas, no family could come over immediately and help. Each night when I returned to my hotel room across the street from the hospital, I would check the mail slot for my room hoping I had received messages of love and support from home. Usually the box was full. One night as I climbed the stairs to my room, I saw, sitting in front of the door, a small vase holding an arrangement of flowers that had been sent by my sister-in-law, Katherine. What an impact this small, thoughtful gift made on my life, on that day, in that time.

"It is always good to know, if only in passing,
a charming human being; it refreshes our lives
like flowers and woods and clear brooks."

—George Eliot

Drunken Carnations

Before becoming a full-time floral designer, I was employed in the medical field, working in home health. Most of my patients were very ill. Although I tried to give them comfort, it was usually they who inspired me. I was often given significant insights into compassion, love, and faith.

One special patient was Mr. Jim. He appeared quite gruff, but was actually a very tenderhearted man. He loved his garden and his flowers. On his good days, I would find him in the early morning sitting out in his yard amid their beauty. His favorite plants, and mine, were his fragrant pink mini carnations. They lined his driveway and completely filled the flower bed. Once, after I had driven in and stepped from my car, their lovely scent surrounding me, I stood there taking it in. Mr. Jim yelled out to me, "What are you doing—getting drunk on my carnations?" I had to smile. I probably did look as though I were getting drunk on the sweet fragrance—and enjoying every minute of it!

Not long after that, Mr. Jim proudly handed me a box filled with carnation plants he had carefully dug from his flower bed. I planted them in my driveway flower bed, just as he had. He said that now I could get "drunk" in my own yard.

The following spring Mr. Jim was very ill. When his carnations bloomed, he was no longer able to go out and smell their sweet fragrance. Each morning when I made my daily visit, I would pick a carnation from his flower bed and lay it on his pillow. He would enjoy its fragrance, and smile. Even during his last days, when he would be sleeping as I arrived, I would leave the carnation. I knew that when he found it his mind would travel to a beautiful, sweet place.

Now as I look through my own garden, I let it bring back special memories. A velvety red rosebush from Sicily given to me by a patient twenty years ago when I was first married, lilies from a customer as a kind thank-you, a rose planted by a loving neighbor from a cutting in her yard, and, of course, most prominent and most fragrant of all—my "drunken" carnations.

Jody Ondrus

Take one and a half dozen carnations in your hands and grasp firmly so that the heads of the flowers are all at the same height. Secure the flowers under the heads until they form a ball. Use a green chenille stem or pipe cleaner to twist under the flower heads and a second one to twist around the bottoms of the stems to keep them in place. Trim all the stems into one length and immediately insert the bunch into a container that holds fresh floral foam. Embellish container with a bow, and continue to add water daily.

Flowers are nature's jewels, with whose wealth
she decks her summer beauty.

—*George Croly*

DESERT BLOOMS

I lived for eight years in the middle of one of the driest places on earth, a place little known until the CNN cameras blazoned its name across our television screens during the Gulf War: Riyadh, in the middle of the kingdom of Saudi Arabia.

Having come from the green fields of England, my prospects for lush vegetation were, I felt, to be restricted to a few palm trees. How wrong I was! A mutual love of flowers brought together a varied group of people from around the world whose lives were enriched as friendships blossomed. We called ourselves "The Riyadh International Flower Group." Truly an international bouquet, our members were from Japan, the Philippines, Korea, Singapore, Germany, Malaysia, China, Thailand, Brazil, Holland, the United States, and, of course, England.

Throughout my life, flowers have reminded me of people—fuschias for my father, daffodils for my sister, roses for my grandmother, lily of the valley for my mother. My friends in the flower group reminded me of different flowers because of the way they spoke about them or shared the way they arranged them. Whenever I see orchids, I see the smiling face of my Singaporean friend, Irene, with her delicate, fragile features. Vibrant red and yellow tulips standing tall and proud evoke Ely from Holland. Hibiscus flowers bring back memories of lovely Sue from Malaysia. Tania, with her extravagant, colorful lifestyle, is just like the mimosa blossoms of Brazil. From Japan, Mareko's explanation of the bonsai tree still makes me gasp with wonderment.

I remember one Good Friday in March as our Land Rover headed out of the city toward the desert for a nature walk. We led the way as eight other overland vehicles, gathered from various compounds around the city, fell in behind. Our guide was an Englishman I had first met four years previously on a visit to a farm on the outskirts of Riyadh. John had been in the Middle East for many years when I arrived. As far as I know, he is still there, cultivating the dry earth for the local sheiks. His expert knowledge of the flora and fauna of the desert was invaluable to a group such as ours as we headed toward our destination.

As we drove over bumpy terrain, I wondered how we would ever find our way back without John, who seemed to be the only one, beside the occasional bedouin, who knew of this place at this particular time of year.

Finally, we reached our destination and formed our vehicles in a circle. Iced drinks were grabbed from coolers as I handed around hot cross buns made especially for us by a local baker. Once we had refreshed ourselves, John started to tell us about his adventures in the desert and how he had come upon this particular spot. As he spoke, we followed him, and it was then that the treasures of the place were revealed to us.

We looked down at our feet and there was a perfectly formed orchid-type flower, farther on a spray of yellow daisy-type flowers. The afternoon sped by and it was only when it was time to go, having to get back to the confines of the city before dark, that we realized we had found twenty-three different types of flowers, each one a little jewel to be treasured for it had survived despite the lack of water and the searing heat of the desert. Each one was a survivor who had found just the right spot at just the right time to flourish. Another week and this area would once again be dry and desolate, and these tiny faces straining toward the light would be no more. But we had found the crack in the door of time and for us this was truly a day the desert bloomed.

Gail Fletcher-Cooke

Avoid feeding garden roses in the fall. Feeding will encourage new growth, which is especially vulnerable to drying winter winds, ice, sudden freezes, and subzero temperatures. Once garden roses go dormant, cut them back to about waist height to prevent winds from haphazardly snapping off the canes.

These roses under my window make no reference to former roses or to better ones; they are what they are; they exist with God today. There is no time to them. There is simply the rose; it is perfect in every moment of existence.

—*Ralph Waldo Emerson*

The Privilege of Giving Roses

"The Privilege of the Platform" was the theme I chose the year I was honored to be president of the National Speakers Association, an organization made up of four thousand professional speakers. Choosing a logo that would reflect that theme was a real challenge. I finally chose two symbols that I felt best portrayed the awesome privilege we have on the platforms we grace. First, a trumpet as a reminder of our invitation, the trumpet sound being one that brings people to "hear," and then the rose as a symbol of giving our very best to our audiences as speakers.

I had over a hundred committee chairpersons, board members, and past presidents that I wanted to thank for their participation during my presidency. Our final convention was to be held in Washington, D.C. All members were going to visit the Lincoln Memorial and have dinner at the reflecting pool, so I chose the

Lincoln rosebush as my thank-you and sent one to each person on my team—in advance of the convention. A living gift!

Since that time, I have received scores of thank-yous and touching stories about how those huge red Lincoln roses continue to bloom, bring joy, and remind people of the privilege of leadership. One friend planted her bush next to the driveway between her house and her neighbor's, bribing her neighbor to care for it with her "green thumb," determined that it would not die. Every time she drives into her garage, she smiles and remembers—"The Privilege of the Platform!" Here are some special thank-yous I'd like to share.

From Jim Pancero:

Now . . . I'm a guy, but worse . . . I'm a business guy . . . a real corporate kind of guy. Flowers for me just don't seem to have the emotional impact that they have for other, more normally balanced individuals. But Naomi's roses were different. Naomi's gift of roses transcended the idea of just giving flowers as a gift. Sending a rosebush to her fellow board members as a thank-you was more than just sending us flowers. Her gift reaffirmed the values she worked to communicate during her year as president. Every time I look at her rosebush gift, even when it is only the trimmed, bared stems of winter, I don't see flowers, I see a year of leadership communicating a vision and direction I am encouraged to follow in both my personal and professional lives.

Her gift accomplished what I see as the real value of giving flowers. It isn't the plant that's important, but the emotions and message the flowers represent. I hope your next gift of flowers to a person important in your life is also able to communicate the power of your feelings and beliefs.

From Nido Qubein:

We planted Naomi's gift in our garden. It was only a couple of brown stems, but after we fed and watered it, the leaves and buds emerged one by one amid its thorns. A beautiful red rose opened up and towered over the bush, its scent evoking the memories of friendship.

Whenever my wife, Mariana, cuts the roses, she thinks of Naomi's thoughtfulness and how much a rosebush is like life. It may contain thorns, but if one is patient, one will find beautiful roses emerging. The roses always remind us that among the hardships in life there are beautiful rewards.

From Liz Curtis Higgs:

Imagine receiving an incredible rosebush when you have not two, but ten brown thumbs. I was thrilled with the generosity of the gift, but scared silly about what to do with it. Fretting over the gift, wondering how in the world I could do it justice when I make silk plants wilt with a single touch, I noticed my office manager regarding it with longing in her eyes.

"Where are you going to put that?" Her voice, and a lengthy sigh, told me all I needed to know. She was afraid I would kill it within a week's time.

"There are lots of corners of our garden that need brightening." I looked at her closely. "Of course, it might really be something in your garden, with your other beautiful roses, eh?"

She gazed at the rosebush. "Sure would."

"Then let's plant it there." I beamed at her. "Correction. Why don't you, oh keeper of ten green thumbs, plant it there yourself?"

So she did just that, planting it in a sunny spot where it blooms to this day, alive and well, a graceful reminder of the beauty of friendship.

From Emory Austin:

When I saw the rosebush, I thought, "What an absolutely perfect gift—both from Naomi and from the Creator."

We are so "privileged," to use Naomi's chosen word, to hold microphones all over the world and to hold in our eyes, hands, and hearts the inspiration that comes from the stunning beauty of a perfect flower. Our rosebush has become more stunning, year by year, as it flourishes in our yard. It has exploded with buds that become full-blown red roses every spring, summer, and fall since we lovingly put it right at the corner of our home. It's the last thing I see when I leave to visit with yet another client. It's the first thing I see when I return home.

Red roses. Naomi's challenge to all of us. Beauty and responsibility all at the same time. Words can plant seeds and blossom just as the roses do. Through changing times we can count on both to make a difference. A poem on my refrigerator by an unknown writer puts it this way:

And then the day came
When the choice to remain tight in a bud
Became more painful
Than the risk it took to blossom.

Buds become blossoms just as nature intends. Words planted will bear even more beautiful fruit. And the privilege of it is ours. Thank you for reminding us, Naomi!

Naomi Rhode

Love is like a beautiful flower
which I may not touch,
but whose fragrance makes
the garden a place
of delight just the same.

—*Helen Keller*

Boy Meets Girl and Flowers

When did I first become aware of flowers? My second year in high school. Oh, I had seen flowers before that, but the meaning that flowers can have for people, and especially for the female of the species, had never dawned on me.

The big awakening came when one of my friends informed me that I must buy a corsage for my sophomore prom date. How to go about this? I was told to first find out the color of her dress so that I could buy flowers that would complement it. Then I had to determine if this was to be a wrist corsage or just a regular one—which would be pinned above the left breast. I thought I would like to pin a regular corsage above her breast. Regrettably, I learned that that was forbidden territory for us boys, and that the mother usually did the pinning. So, I settled on a wrist corsage of red roses.

I was delighted to see the pleased look on her face when she took the roses out of the box. She, of course, presented me with the customary white carnation, carnations being more manly than roses. The evening progressed nicely and by the time I walked her to the door at the end of the night I would have to say that my first encounter with purchasing a corsage for a formal date was a total success.

Over the remainder of my high school and college years, I bought many more rose corsages, figuring I should stay with a winning formula. One would have thought that the lesson I learned would stay with me throughout my life, but, unfortunately, that was not the case. Flowers certainly played a role in winning my wife's hand in marriage, but over time the special things we do to win someone's hand disappear when that hand is won.

As I think back over the years, I realize that it shouldn't have to be a special event to warrant the giving of flowers. If I had my life to live over, I would give my wife more roses—many more.

Kenneth H. Killen

Making a Profit

Stan was my twin's fraternity brother. A constant entrepreneur, according to my brother John, Stan never missed a trick for finding a way to make a buck. Back then, swept up in my '60s "attitude" of peace and love, I regarded Stan with disdain. So much for false impressions.

When it was homecoming at Emory University in Atlanta and time for the formal occasions, Stan, true to his nature, decided to peddle roses up and down fraternity row. "Make Your Date a Queen-for-a-Day," he would shout as he knocked on doors.

Unfortunately, Stan was overly optimistic about how many flowers he could sell. Dozens remained. Stan found his way to downtown Atlanta, and for a full day watched for women walking down the street. Oh, not the sweet young things with shapely figures and miniskirts. No, Stan watched for the elderly, the homely, the less than lovely ones. Then, smiling, he went up to each one, extended a rose, and proclaimed, "You're beautiful!" With that, he vanished into the street scene.

Did Stan lose money? Probably. But he gained so much more. As for me, he left a lasting impression—of generosity.

Eileen McDargh

One should learn to enjoy the neighbor's garden,
however small; the roses straggling over the fence,
the scent of lilacs drifting across the road.

—Henry Van Dyke

Teacher, My Dog Ate My Book

I had a frantic woman on the other end of the phone wanting to send her neighbor flowers. It seems that the neighbor had loaned her a book to read. My customer asked if I had heard the old excuse for not turning in homework: "Teacher, my dog ate my book." Well, guess what, the woman's dog had eaten the back cover off the loaned book, and she thought the best way to "smooth over" the incident was to send flowers. The book was a used, out-of-print edition, and so it could not be replaced.

She asked me to put on the card, "Tigger enjoyed your book as much as I did!" Luckily, the neighbor had a sense of humor and the flowers did the trick! All was forgiven.

Jim Somppi

Fragrance is the strongest and
most mysterious of the sensual pleasures
that gardens offer. . . . Each of us has
our talisman fragrances, odors that magically
obliterate the intervening days and
years between ourselves as we are now and
ourselves as we once were.
Fragrance makes us feel
at home in our gardens,
and our gardens make
us truly at home in the world.

—*Allen Lacy*

Lost and Found

It seems that when you're pushing eighty, you start to lose things like keys, teeth, hearing, even the sense of smell. But what do these have to do with flowers? Well, there's a lovely magnolia tree outside my window filled with large blossoms that I can't smell. I even go to the local florist to admire the beauty of the flowers, but I can't smell the fragrance of the cut flowers and plants there.

Memory loss is another thing. I can't remember to keep plants happy. My neighbor has Christmas poinsettia blooming until June; mine are dead by New Year's. I'm no longer a gardener, that's for sure. I now have silk flower arrangements and silk plants. I even bought one with a few brown leaves to look as if it were truly mine.

In spite of my losses, this past Christmas I received a box from my dear granddaughter, Debbie. Opening it, I found something that looked like a big onion with lots of strings hanging from it. Needless to say, I took it to the florist to have it potted.

Since folks reminded me to water it, it began to grow. First there were two, then four, and finally seven huge pink-and-white amaryllis blooms at one time. A miracle? I'd say I found some things that love returned to me.

Ruth Kuhnle

Mix 8 drops of immortelle, a floral essential oil available at health food stores, and 30 drops of lavender to create an oil for sunburn. As a disinfectant, mix 1 3/4 fluid ounces of immortelle, 1 3/4 fluid ounces of St. John's wort oil, and 1 3/4 ounces of aloe vera oil.

Collecting, dispensing, singing, there I wander with them.
Plucking something for tokens, tossing toward whoever is
near me. Here, lilac, with a branch of pine. Here, out of
my pocket, some moss which I pull'd off a live-oak in
Florida as it hung trailing down. Here, some pinks
and laurel leaves, and a handful of sage . . .

— *Walt Whitman*

LAURA

One very hot summer day, Laura arrived. This beautiful three-month-old baby girl turned me into an instant mom. Flowers and frills arrived with her, gifts from friends and family. As the years passed, Laura grew up thinking that flowers were the ultimate gift, and she gave them to me whenever possible. At first she "borrowed" from her grandma's garden and even from the neighbors, being just a toddler at the time. We moved to sunny California when she was six, and our bountiful gardens put bouquets at her fingertips. She became my personal "florist" for the frequent dinners we hosted, and continued to present me with gifts of flowers she had picked and arranged herself.

During her tenth summer, she gave me what turned out to be the most potentially expensive birthday gift I have ever received. We were at my father's cabin, deep in the woods in northern Wisconsin. A well-meaning friend from the city took Laura canoeing through the calm, quiet beds of wild rice that surrounded Dad's cabin on a point of land jutting out into the water. It happened to be my birthday, and sometime during the afternoon Laura returned from her canoe trip and came running excitedly up the path with a large bouquet in hand. Although I had always taught my children not to pick wildflowers, I guess I slipped up on the wild "water" flowers. Her latest gift was made up of several rare and protected water lilies. If you know the rules on that one, you will know that I was looking at a bouquet worth several hundred dollars in fines. I was aghast, and I clumsily showed it.

My poor daughter read my face and burst into tears. I smoothed it over as best I could, put the flowers in water, and hoped and prayed that the "wildflower police" hadn't seen Laura. (Fortunately, no one came to call.)

Laura's now an adult, and the era of her "borrowed" flowers has passed into creating a home abounding in her own flowers and plants that she tends and shares generously. She has added another element to her gifts for me. Since she is now a mother herself, I get to "borrow" grandchildren.

Loretta Daum Byrne

HIDE-AND-SEEK FLOWERS

I remember a Mother's Day, long ago, when my two youngest daughters were ages six and seven. I awoke that morning to find little notes left for me to read and follow their trail through the house. They led me to a note in the fireplace that said, "Look in the oven." The note in the oven said, "Look in the kitchen." The final note led me to the family room. As I entered, my two youngest daughters jumped out from behind the doorway and yelled, "Happy Mother's Day." Held in their small hands was a little petunia plant. It was the most beautiful gift I have ever received, for the joy and adoration in their faces made me realize what a lucky mother I was to have such loving, thoughtful children.

Betty Valle

Send a packet of seeds, a pot, and some dirt to a child, grandchild, niece, or nephew in another city. Ask them to plant their flower while you plant one of yours. Watching them grow together will be a reminder of the love you share across the miles.

I will no longer permit the avid and eager eye to steal away my whole attention. I will learn to enjoy more completely all the varied wonders of the earth.

—*David Grayson*

Flowers Feed the Soul

In November of 1995, I enjoyed the life-saving experience of open-heart surgery. In September of 1996, I enjoyed the life-saving experience of radical prostate surgery. Each time my room overflowed with beautiful flowers from friends far and near. While I was grateful for the developments of modern medicine, I was inspired by the spirit-saving experiences of nature's bountiful loveliness—created by God to cheer us.

Arnold "Nick" Carter

There seems to be a misconception that the gift of flowers is only for women. The truth is, men love to receive flowers as well. Once, I was to be gone on a business trip for several days. My husband was going to have to carry the burden of not only his duties, but mine as well. I wanted him to know how much I appreciated him, so I arranged with my local florist to deliver flowers the day after I left.

At first he was a bit taken aback by the gift and his macho side came forward and said, "Flowers, for me! Why?" But as the hours and days went on, he realized how much he really appreciated the gift. It was the first time, he said, that he was ever able to appreciate the beauty of flowers and know the design was made just for him.

Many a visitor has departed from my garden
with a handful of sweet smelling leaves
carefully treasured in
handkerchief or pocket.

—*Rosetta E. Clarkson*

Floral Comfort

Flowers! I love them all—from the glamorous orchid to the most humble wildflower! Flowers refresh my spirit and make me smile. My idea of the ultimate luxury is to have fresh flowers in every room, every day.

The delight I find in flowers was passed on to me by my mother and grandmother; both loved to grow flowers and arrange beautiful bouquets. Thanks to them, I have "comfort flowers" as well as "comfort foods." Flowering quince and petunias remind me of Nannie; irises, roses, and moss roses bring memories of my mother's artistic flower beds and arrangements. The sight and scent of any of these special blooms make me feel content, loved, and protected.

Betsy Edwards

"Just living is not enough," said the butterfly.
"One must have sunshine, freedom, and a little flower."

—*Hans Christian Andersen*

Will I Ever Have a Geranium That Will Last?

Across the street from our store where I lived as a child, in three rooms behind the customer counter, was the local church. It was the only social center we had, and we were present every time it opened. Once a year we had "Children's Sunday," a special day in June when we received awards for perfect attendance and were given recognition for any honor we might have earned throughout the year. It was a dress-up day when we happily put on the best we had because we knew we would be called up front by name. I remember the excitement as we met in our Sunday school rooms and were given our instructions on how to behave in "big church."

We marched as a quiet, awestruck army and dutifully took our assigned seats. Miss Badden, our perpetual Sunday school superintendent, stood at the appointed time and walked to the platform. She read off the winners' names, and we'd walk forward with dignity. No one ran or giggled. This was church.

The most exciting part of the ceremony came at the end of the service: the giving out of geraniums. The platform was ringed with little pots of bright red geraniums, and we knew from the start that we would each get one. The toddlers went first, and I can still see my brother Ron's eyes as he brought his first geranium up the aisle to his seat. My other brother, Jim, would give me a proud grin as he passed by, and then it would be my turn. I always wished I had a prettier dress or curlier hair, but at least I was going to get a geranium. Miss Badden would hand me the little clay pot with one lonely geranium at the top of a long stalk. I would have a flower of my own.

I'd take my little pot home, and each year I'd vow to make my geranium last forever. One year it fell off the porch railing where I'd put it for decoration. Once it shriveled up and died in our dark kitchen. Another time I planted it outside in the hard dirt, and a hurried customer stepped on it. "Sorry," he called back to me as he hastened on, unaware that he had trampled the only flower I'd have for another year. I sat on the steps and wondered, "Will I ever have a geranium that will last? Will I ever have any flowers?"

I realize now why my favorite hymn was always "In the Garden." The words expressed my childhood dream that I might trade the blacktop and gas pump at the store for a garden. I wanted to find an Eden full of geraniums. I wanted to "come to the garden alone while the dew is still on the roses." I wanted to walk with Him and talk with Him and have Him tell me, "I am His own." When I chose this hymn for my baptism back in 1966, I didn't realize that my choice sprouted from that inner childhood longing for a garden full of fresh flowers—or at least one little lonely geranium.

Once, in thinking about my childhood with no flowers and my desire for some touch of beauty, I asked my husband, Fred, "Could I have a little pot of geraniums?"

"You can have all the geraniums you want," he answered. "You can have geraniums on the wall and on the curtains. You can have pots at the front door and window boxes full of them. You don't need to cry for a geranium ever again." And I did get my geraniums: on the wallpaper, on the curtains, in pots at the front and back doors, and in my flower gardens.

Florence Littauer

Not only will flowers provide beauty and fragrance, some are even edible and can add a delectable touch to your evening meal. Some of the most popular edible flowers and their flavors include calendula, which tastes buttery; chives, which are oniony; mint and pansy, which taste minty; nasturtium, which tastes spicy; rose and violet, which are floral tasting; and marigold and sage, which taste herbal.

My garden, with its silence and pulses of fragrance
that come and go on the airy undulations,
affects me like sweet music. Care stops at the gates and
gazes at me wistfully through the bars.

—*Alexander Smith*

Captive Audience

I was teaching basic horticulture rehabilitation to inmates at a local correctional facility, and tonight, for our second lesson, we were going to be talking about plant anatomy. The students were an interesting assortment of about ten men ranging in age from their early twenties to their late fifties. I wasn't quite sure what they were expecting to get out of the class, but I made a quick stop by the flower shop and asked for some old flowers that I thought I would use in my demonstrations. The woman gave me some semi-spent roses and mums and some filler. I also took some boxwood, juniper, cedar, pine, and spruce. A quick whirl past an Ohio Buckeye provided some dormant twigs.

As I drove to the prison, I thought about how my students might enjoy getting some fresh flowers and felt I had a prize in the long-stemmed red roses I had been given. Clutching my bag of goodies, I set up my little class in a room that doubled as a chapel. My props were a pulpit, a large brass cross, and a graphic painting of Jesus nailed to a cross. I'm Jewish, and I thought, "If only my mother could see me now."

The men arrived accompanied by three staff members. As we began with a review of the previous week's material, I was surprised by their enthusiasm and obvious pleasure at seeing me, and they were eager to show that they had done their homework. When we moved on to this week's lesson, I began by showing them detailed drawings of basic plant parts. We focused on stems, leaves, and flowers. I passed out the assorted greenery and noticed that they couldn't get enough of the smells and textures. One man even commented, "You can chew on these pine needles!" They all took a chomp, but I cautioned them not to be so eager to eat their samples.

Passing out the Buckeye twig, I pointed out the leaf scales, bundle scars, and lenticels. They studied their twigs intently. Then came the flowers. Each student was given a long-stemmed red rose. Hands reached out as if to say "Gimme." While I was explaining the alternate leaf arrangement, I could tell it was the flower that had captured their attention. They were feeling it, smelling it, thinking about it. They were remembering and learning. "So," I teased, "when was the last time another guy gave you roses?" They laughed but said nothing. And in that moment I understood why they were so captivated by these ordinary leaves, sticks, and flowers. For some, it had been months since they had been outside. Confined at night to their stark cells, this glimpse of nature was indeed a treat.

As the class came to an end, it was time to turn in the samples. Plant material was considered "contraband" and was not allowed into their cells. The men clutched their roses and tried to roll them up into their papers. I felt that to take them away was to cross over into what could only be "cruel and unusual punishment." The room fell silent. The corrections officers looked back and forth at each other and finally at me. The inmates held on tightly to their posies. "Okay," I said, "you can keep your flowers as study aids." The tension vanished. The men grinned and began to file out of the room. "See ya next week, Chuck!" they chimed. I felt great.

Chuck Levine

LIFE LESSONS

4·

THE EARTH LAUGHS IN FLOWERS.

—Ralph Waldo Emerson

ANSWERING A PRAYER

On June 12, 1995, I received the call that no parent wants to receive. The Christiana Hospital emergency room was calling to tell my husband and me that our son had been involved in a very serious auto accident; they needed our permission to continue life-saving procedures on him. Unless you are on the receiving end of this kind of call, you will never know the feeling of hearing those words. Our son was in critical condition and not expected to live. On the third day, the head of the trauma team, with tears in his eyes, asked my husband and me if we believed in God. We both answered yes immediately. "Well," he said, "I suggest you pray as hard as you can because we've done everything, and I just don't know if Joey is going to make it."

It wasn't that we hadn't already been praying for days, but we now prayed to God to please send our son back to us. Weary and spent, we went home very late that night to try to get some sleep. I don't know what made me even think of my poor, neglected plants, but I decided to water them, praying as I did so. When I got to my gardenia, having tried for many, many years to get it to bloom, there was the biggest, most beautiful blossom rising from its top. I couldn't believe my eyes. After all those years, it appeared—beautiful and fragrant—all of a sudden. I knew it had to be a message from God that my son would survive. And he did.

He suffers from traumatic brain injury as a result of the accident, but despite his physical and memory deficits, my son won two scholarships in his senior year, he was able to graduate with his class, and he is now in college, part-time and struggling, but still getting As and Bs. He is very active in promoting awareness of people with disabilities and has been written up in numerous local newspapers for his valiant fight to recover and help others.

Every year, my son is stronger and closer to walking than the year before. And every year for the past three years since the accident, my gardenia produces a single bloom.

Kathy Tridente

The gardenia is an evergreen shrub with flowers that will bloom in either white or ivory. Each flower lasts two to five days. They should be cut as soon as the blooms are fully open. Gardenia petals bruise easily when handled. They can be floated in water, without their foliage, for a centerpiece.

The gardens of my youth were
fragrant gardens
and it is their sweetness rather than
their patterns or
their furnishings that
I now most clearly recall.

—*Louise Beebe Wilder*

Seeing Honeysuckle

When I was about thirteen, I took our family friend Ms. Arnold out for a canoe ride. What was unusual about the adventure was that Ms. Arnold weighed about three hundred pounds, had never been in a canoe in her life, and was blind. At the time, the worst thing that I could imagine was to be blind. I was also fearful of having the canoe overturn and having Ms. Arnold drown, or drown me as I attempted to pull her out.

Ms. Arnold, on the other hand, was having the time of her life. She kept up a constant barrage of questions about what was on the shore, could I see any fish, or how far were we from the frog that was croaking. Then, in the middle of all her questions, she told me to be quiet. She asked if I could see "it." See "it"? What was she talking about, she was blind! She repeated her question, "Can you see it, the honeysuckle, can you see it?" At that point I looked around, and sure enough, there was a small clump of honeysuckle about 150 feet from the boat at the top of a small embankment. There are many ways of "seeing," and Ms. Arnold taught me the importance of being open to the unique abilities of those around me. Ms. Arnold and her lesson are brought back every time I smell honeysuckle.

John O. Boyd III

I know spring has surely arrived when I see the yellow honeysuckle blossoms burst forth from their stems to brighten the awakening earth. Their aroma is fabulous, especially in the evening. Plant honeysuckle near a wall that catches the end-of-the-day light—then be sure to sit near it in the evening as you relax and unwind.

Gardening is an exercise in optimism.
Sometimes, it is the triumph of hope
over experience.

—*Marina Schinz*

A Garden of the Spirit

I love gardening, digging in the ground, watching the plants grow and the flowers bloom. For years I nurtured a cottage garden in my small yard where we live, on the central coast of California. The wonderful climate here allows for a garden that blooms from January to November. Several years ago we bought a summer home in Colorado, and I found myself putting all my energy into the concentrated blooming season high up in the Rockies. I looked forward to planting and watching the abundant flowers each summer, and sharing their beauty with some special friends. However, being gone during the summer necessitated changing our landscaping in California from "cottage garden" to "drought-tolerant" ground cover and shrubs including as many winter-blooming plants as possible.

As we were preparing to leave for Colorado this year, I was diagnosed with breast cancer. My treatments required us to stay in California for the summer. It's peculiar how we can focus on silly things when we are facing a life-threatening situation. My most difficult obstacle was giving up my garden and gardening friends in Colorado. My heart grieved for all those wonderful blossoms, *and* I was stuck with my "drought-tolerant" yard in California. Even though they commiserated with me, my family thought all of this fuss was of secondary importance to my getting immediate treatment. I agreed, but I still missed the thought of my garden.

Well, God knows the desires of our hearts, and apparently He knew the importance of my garden. This had been the year of El Niño, and El Niño brought so much rain, and the birds dropped so many seeds, that plants that had never been a part of our garden started sprouting all over the yard. We had a summer of the most beautiful "cottage garden" our yard had ever seen. Flowers of all kinds bloomed abundantly from the middle of

May until early September. The low fences wore the vibrant yellows, oranges, and reds of nasturtiums. The ground covers flowered with pinks and purples, and the shrubs of lavender and rosemary bloomed abundantly with purples and blues. The few roses I rescued overflowed with yellow and peach blooms, daisies cropped up in corners, irises that had never bloomed erupted with every color imaginable, and the foxgloves shot their glorious spires six feet into the sky. Volunteer sunflowers smiled at us along the sunny driveway, while fragrant violets, violas, and freesias carpeted the shady spots. Even the camellias and azaleas bloomed out of season! Every time I walked outside, my spirits soared and my heart filled with joy to see my bounteous flowers and breathe in their mingling scents. Throughout the summer, as I went through the ups and downs of treatment, my unexpected garden gave me the special peace and comfort that comes from the knowledge that God is indeed in control and provides more abundantly than I could ever imagine.

Debi Linker

Hummingbirds are one of my favorite birds. I love the way their bodies reflect the light. As they hover delicately in the air, they appear to be little fairies. The best way to attract them is with plants that are profusely covered with sweet nectar flowers. Try some of these: butterfly bush, hibiscus, azalea, weigela, honeysuckle, hollyhock, columbine, fuschia, impatiens, salvia, and phlox.

Flowers from Nepal

Mom always has flowers of some kind on the kitchen table or near the window so that their fragrance can be blown into the house by afternoon breezes. When I arrived home from school, I was greeted by either the aroma of spaghetti sauce cooking or the smell of hyacinths or roses or daisies or whatever flower inspired Mom. I could almost tell what kind of mood she was in by the kind of flower she displayed. I reached the point where I took Mom's flowers for granted. I just always expected them to be there.

During a recent summer, I spent six weeks in Nepal with a sociology program, through Miami University. Four of those six weeks were spent in downtown Kathmandu, perhaps the dirtiest city I have ever been in. Trapped in the valley by the surrounding Himalayas, a constant beige haze hovered over the city. Diesel-burning clunker cars whizzed by on dusty dirt roads covered in trash and animal dung. The rivers were hopelessly polluted. Surrounded by such squalid conditions for a solid month, I found my thoughts drifting back to Mom's flowers on the kitchen table. For the first time, I really appreciated the flowers that then seemed so far away.

As I delved deeper into Nepali culture, I discovered that flowers were a very important part of their lifestyle as well. On Saturday, their holy day, Nepalis go to Hindu and Buddhist temples to worship their gods and goddesses. Outside the temples, peddlers set up tables selling flowers to be used as gifts to the gods. The flowers are an expression of devotion, a tangible way to express intangible faith.

Flowers have a place of honor in temples, and in homes as well. The final two weeks of my trip was a home stay with a Nepali family, where I got to see firsthand how important flowers were to them. I stayed with the Lakhes, an extremely loving family of five. The father was a pharmacist employed by the Nepali government. The mother, whom I called Bhaauju (pronounced "bowjoo"), worked as a teller at one of Kathmandu's few banks. I also had three sisters—Rehna, Reema, and Neha (weird for me because I grew up with only one brother). In the kitchen of their small house, they had made a shrine honoring

Hindu gods. Such shrines are common in Hindu homes and are a very sacred element of their faith. Every morning Bhaauju would wake up early, and while ringing a high-pitched bell would pray to the gods in front of the little shrine.

Never once did I see the shrine without flowers adorning each statue. Bhaauju took great care decorating the statues with flowers from the plants growing outside her home. Huge red flowers and tiny blue ones were placed in the figures' hands and at their feet. Every few days Bhaauju would pick new flowers to replace those that had withered. No worship would begin until the flowers were properly replaced because they were a way for her to keep her faith fresh, to continually show her gods that she was doing what was required of her by the Hindu religion.

When it came time to say good-bye to my Nepali family, we were all sad that our time together had come to an end. Nepalis are much better at good-bye than Americans. Bhaauju sat me down in the family room to perform a small farewell ceremony. Surrounded by the rest of the family, she presented me with a flower bouquet made with flowers from their garden. Each variety of flower they grew was a part of the bouquet. And what a fragrance! The aroma enveloped me like a hug from a close friend. I waved good-bye to my family with my duffel bag in one hand and the bouquet in the other. As I rode across the city in a taxi, the aroma of the flowers kept my thoughts on the family I might never see again until I recalled Mom's flowers and understood the universality of the natural beauty of my world and all its people.

Joe Lamancusa Jr.

Roses blooming and growing are a fond memory of my childhood. My dad was an absolute genius, or so it seemed to me, in growing them. I remember that he had all kinds of roses in pots sitting on the sills of the basement windows. Once he even took a rose stem from a bouquet of roses my sister had received from one of her boyfriends. He grafted it and prepared it in such a way that it began to grow as its own bush. As I look back, I can see that my father found a great deal of comfort and stability in planting, weeding, and cultivating a showcase of roses. During the war, as a seventeen-year-old youth, he had spent time in a Nazi work camp. The horrors and atrocities he witnessed and experienced were with him throughout his life. But all of that was forgotten when he nurtured and cared for his prizes—beautiful roses.

June brings tulips, lilies, roses
Fills the children's hands with posies.

—*Traditional rhyme*

Neighborly Tulips

My mother had the greenest thumb I've ever encountered, and as a child I was well aware, at a very early age, of her love for flowers. That's why one beautiful spring day on my way home from first grade, I picked her a giant bouquet of red tulips . . . from a neighbor's flower bed! My mother marched me back to the neighbor, tulips in hand, to fess up to the misdeed. This was a neighbor we had not yet met and who had no children of her own. Oh my, was I afraid as we rang her doorbell to apologize. But that day the angels smiled at my youthful innocence, and all turned out better than I could have imagined. In no time, the neighbor and my mother became the best of friends, exchanging bulbs and plantings over the years. Not too long after, we had a tulip bed even grander than the original. Best of all, I got to keep all the tulips I had picked that day!

Shea Szachara

Cut tulips continue to "grow" after they are cut. Even after the stems are inserted into floral arrangements, they continue to elongate. Insert the tulips a little deeper in the design, then if the tulip grows longer than is visually appealing, remove the flower, recut the stem, and insert it back into the design. If your tulip stems are too curved for use, wrap the bunch fairly tightly in paper and insert in a container of cool water. Let them sit for at least one hour before arranging.

The name "daisy" comes from the Old English phrase "day's eye" because some daisies open their petals in the morning, revealing the center disk, and close them each night.

Bouquet of Hope

My love affair with daisies began in 1972 when I was a child of twelve. I was away from home, attending a church-sponsored youth camp. By Tuesday, I was starting to feel a little homesick. On Wednesday, our leaders had us get on a bus to go on a little field trip. We drove for over two hours to a new campground site. This, we were told, would be where future camps would be held.

We marveled at the unblemished beauty of nature. There were grassy meadows, rolling hills, and wild, pure-white daisies growing amid the high grasses. As the boys explored the hills and valleys, we girls got busy picking bouquets of wild daisies.

When we returned to our old camp's barracks (some would call it a dorm room, but this was a wooden, dingy room filled with at least ten bunk beds), we scavenged around looking for soda bottles that could be rinsed out and used as vases. When we ran out of bottles, we looked for cups and other containers that would serve.

Those daisies brightened up the place, especially for me. By Saturday, when it was time to go home, my daisies still looked as fresh and alive as the day I had picked them. Once I had returned home, my daisies continued to live through the following week.

From that point on, daisies became my symbol of hope, my link to reality, my encourager. When I've hit rough times in my life, just seeing a daisy reminds me that I can make it.

That symbolism and my attachment to daisies were put to the test in 1994. After struggling with depression on and off for over four years, I hit a point where I didn't want to face tomorrow. I plummeted so low that I considered suicide. As a result, I was hospitalized in a psychiatric ward.

Then, it arrived. There before me sat a beautiful full basket of white daisies. My mind raced back to standing in that open field full of wild daisies and remembering how homesick I had felt. Those daisies, those wonderful and beautiful daisies, inspired me to keep going. They convinced me that if a fragile petaled flower could maintain the stamina to survive, even after being stripped from its home, that I, too, could survive. At that moment, I knew I would survive the depression that enveloped me.

And I did. I became a participant in my recovery. I read everything about depression that I could get my hands on. I entered counseling. I took antidepressants. But most important, I asked questions and challenged those who were supposed to have all the answers. As it turned out—with my active participation being the key factor—the cause of my depression was related to a hormone imbalance and wasn't fueled solely on its own as most major depressions are.

Without those daisies, I probably wouldn't be alive to share this today. But because my husband knew me well enough to send me that basket of hope, I grasped the symbolism that had held me up so many times before, and I hung on for dear life.

Penny E. Stone

Before I was married, I really loved daisies. I would pick them wild, buy them fresh, and even asked my dad to grow some for me. In fact, I was so obsessed with daisies that my husband (husband-to-be at the time), called me "Daisy" as a nickname. In the Victorian language of flowers, the daisy means innocence and simplicity. As I think back to that time in my life, I have to say that it certainly was a lot simpler. No family to care for, no job to keep up or bills to pay. I have many more favorite flowers since then, but every time I see a daisy, I think of when my life was simpler. Even the thought relaxes me. To this day, when my husband buys me an impromptu bunch of flowers, he always searches for one that contains at least one daisy. What flower brings back memories of simpler times in your life? Surround yourself with them.

In one myth, Cupid hurries off to a council of the gods on Mount Olympus, carrying a vase of nectar for them to drink. He stumbles and spills the nectar, and it bubbles up from the earth in the form of roses.

MY FATHER'S LANGUAGE OF FLOWERS

For my father, flowers are his language and his love. He is now in his eighties and his career was inspired by his love of flora. Before serving in World War II, he opened a small florist shop. He had to close the shop while he went away to war, but after the war the young newlywed needed a job. Dad signed on in the greenhouses of the local park system, where he would later rise to become director of the entire organization. He was, and remains, a quiet man. Expressing his feelings is difficult for him, but tenderness is in his nature, and presenting a gentle gift of flowers is his usual practice. When I was growing up, he made the abrupt, often misunderstood monosyllabic comments common to men of his generation. Yet I remember well my birthday parties when every "young lady" was given a corsage, handmade by my dad. His poetry was not made of words, but of roots and leaves. I can't remember a time when I didn't know how to look for the king in the Johnny jump ups or how to turn hollyhocks upside down to make elegant ladies.

I have lived in many homes and tended many gardens, and for each my dad has given me newspaper-wrapped offerings of tender shoots so that his love has rooted and taken hold and has left a legacy as we've moved on. Dad has taught me many things, but his lessons in the language of flowers are the ones I prize the most. Now I must be diligent and nurture those delicate "offerings" for my children so that when words become difficult, I can wrap my feelings in soggy newsprint, admonish my children not to overwater, and send them on their way.

Liz Bernstein

Flowers and fruits are always fit presents, flowers,
because they are a proud assertion that a ray
of beauty outvalues all the utilities of the world.

—*Ralph Waldo Emerson*

"Doing Good" with Flowers

I was a newly rejected wife and mother of three. My life had suddenly and painfully been turned upside down, and there were only a few things about which I was sure: I wanted someone to love me, I wanted someone to love my children, and I loved working with flowers.

To my surprise—without any hint or warning—"Mr. Very, Very Right" stepped into my consciousness. His name was Steve, and although we had participated in many church functions together, it was not until he asked the kids and me out for dinner that I had any inkling he was interested. That first night Steve asked me to consider marrying him. I did not yet have any strong feelings for him, but I knew he was a decent and worthy gentleman, so I agreed to consider his proposal.

Over the next couple of months we dated, but unfortunately, the premature timing of Steve's request had a very unsettling effect on me, emotionally, and I could never quite be myself around him again. To my sorrow, just about the time I was falling in love with him, he informed me that his hasty proposal of marriage had been a mistake.

They say hope springs eternal, which is not necessarily a good thing. Over the next year, while I was vigilantly watching the door for Steve's return, he was getting on with his life, which included finding and becoming engaged to another woman.

I had only just heard this news when Steve himself telephoned me and asked, in a genuinely friendly way, if I would "do" the flowers for his wedding. Piercing like an arrow through the tumult of all my clamoring thoughts, one phrase prevailed: "Serve one another." Somehow I managed to eke out a yes, but when I hung up the phone I was nauseated, literally nauseated.

I had said yes to honor my beliefs as a Christian. We are called to "serve one another" and we are called to "do good" to others, even if they hurt us. To be sure, in this case the hurt inflicted was purely unintentional. Throughout the months leading up to the wedding, I poured my whole heart into planning and, at last, arranging those flowers. As I did, all the bitterness, jealousy, and resentment was washed away. I found my healing and my freedom in giving. Flowers were the vehicle by which I could "do good" to Steve and his bride. The wonderful thing about flowers is that they not only provide beauty and joy to the recipients, but they are a great source of pleasure to the preparer as well.

Just a footnote: Steve, his wife, Robin, and I are friends to this day. Although we live in different states, I know that if I ever need them, they will be there for me, and my commitment to them is the same.

Caprice Alicia Baker

Jasmine oil mixes well with rose, neroli, sandalwood, orange, or cypress oil. Mix a capful in a warm bath, turn off the lights, surround the tub with candles, and listen to your favorite soft, relaxing music at the end of a stressful day.

To stand by the beds at sunrise and see the flowers awake is a heavenly delight.

—*Celia Thaxter*

Blossoms on the Communist Block

Her face strained by frustration, Galina leaned into me and said, "We have an expression for times like these. It goes, 'When the lines are long and the pantry is empty, the only way out is laughter.' " We were standing in a long line of people trying to buy food before the shop closed for the day. It was rumored that this place had cheese to sell, but in standard Soviet fashion, there were no guarantees as to the type or freshness of the cheese we might find if we reached the counter before they ran out of this much desired commodity. We had been waiting for more than two hours and had advanced only a few yards since joining the line.

"It's times like these that make me embarrassed to be Russian," she continued, "and for this inconvenience, I must apologize to you." The same irony that had struck me two weeks earlier when I arrived at the airport struck me again. This was not a spy novel, nor was it *Dr. Zhivago*. This was real life in the Soviet city of Moscow, and this proud, gracious woman, who at thirty-one had educated herself well beyond the expectations of her society (and our own) and was fluent in seven languages was much in demand in Moscow's growing international business community.

Yet she was susceptible to feelings of inferiority caused by conditions over which she had absolutely no control. Even more ironic, she was not sorry for herself, but for me, someone who would soon return to a place where everything is readily available and the standard perception of a long grocery line is three or four individuals.

Nevertheless, her choice of expressions worked, and, "the only way out is laughter" soon had me smiling. Indeed, the phrase explained much about what I would observe and experience during my two tours through that volatile region of diversity and change. Never had I been to a place where everyday life was so heavy with dread, and yet never had I been with people so eager to make friends, to share stories, to compare lives, and, above all else, to laugh. There were always funny tales, jokes following jokes, and, of course, there was always the vodka. But it was not until a few days after the long wait at the cheese shop that I discovered something else that was always there to make people laugh, or at least bring a bright smile to the faces of those who had harried lives.

Moscow in August is a hot, humid city alive with smells. Having little in the way of pollution controls, there are what the locals call "lead days and zinc days," and they can tell you which factories are operating and which are not by the way the air smells. Add to this the exhaust of thousands of cars and trucks and you have what the least of our environmentally concerned citizens would call an environmental nightmare. The weeds and grass that grow between the apartment buildings rarely get mowed, so there is the smell of rotting leaves and underbrush. There's road dust, diesel fuel, and Dumpsters overflowing with rotten garbage that can create such a stench that even the cats that live wild in the streets won't go near them.

You travel around the city and for far too long your westernized senses pick up very little except that which is most offensive. But then one day you find yourself walking in one of the many open-air markets that predate the fall of communism and acted as the Soviet Union's introduction to the basics of capitalism. You look at carrots, tomatoes, apples, pears, and cherries and find yourself somewhat surprised that they look exactly like the fruits and vegetables that you find in similar markets at home. You look and touch, and sometimes a grower lets you taste. And then, as if being struck between the eyes, right in that center where the senses lie, other smells hit you; no longer lead or zinc, or any of the other olfactory assaults you've become attuned to. No, suddenly you smell flowers: the sweet fragrance of iris, gladiolus, carnations, and, yes, even the rose!

All dramatics aside, the fragrance of those wonderful blossoms hit me with all the force of a lightning bolt. And, as if that wasn't enough, when I asked Galina where they had all suddenly come from, and why there were so many vendors selling flowers, she simply smiled and said, "Laughter."

"What do you mean?" I asked, a little taken aback.

"They come from all over the republics, and are grown just to create joy and laughter," she explained. "They are perfume and beauty, and are one of those rare things that feed the soul of every living Russian. You find them everywhere. Those who grow them are proud to display them and are complimented when you buy from them. To give them brings much joy, and to get them, well . . . love often follows that tear of joy that comes with flowers."

"You find them in our markets and in our kitchens," she continued. "They become the patterns for our bright summer dresses and our colorful Matruschka, those lovely little wooden dolls you bought for your daughters yesterday. Even in winter you find them knitted on our sweaters and embroidered on our shirts." She looked at me playfully, a sheepish grin coming to her face. "There's another expression that goes, 'Those who believe in God say He made flowers to warm the human heart on cold Russian nights. And' "—she hesitated—" 'those who don't believe in God say He made flowers to warm the human heart on cold Soviet nights!' "

Tom Kumpf

The rose is the oldest domesticated flower known; fossilized imprints found in Florissant, Colorado, indicate that roses existed around 40 million years ago.

Smell is a potent wizard that transports us across thousands of miles and all the years we have lived.

—*Helen Keller*

One Perfect Gardenia

My father was an interior designer, a sensitive and artistic man who loved flowers, but because my mother suffered from numerous allergies, particularly in spring and summer, we never had any flowers in our home. I made crepe paper flowers, but that was all.

We had a small backyard, and when I was thirteen, Dad and I decided to grow some flowers we could enjoy and Mother could see from the kitchen window.

One trash day, our neighbor threw away a lifeless-looking gardenia plant. Dad took it for his own. He bought a gardening book, followed the instructions, and gave it great care. Everyone said it would not grow, it was too far gone. But Dad persisted, and on one bright shiny day that plant produced one perfect gardenia. To this day, when I see, smell, or even hear of that flower, I think of my dad. It seems to represent what he was—hopeful, caring, and persevering. A nice way to learn such lessons.

Ginger Kean Berk

To prevent gardenia blossoms from browning, spray with a mister bottle filled with full-strength lemon juice.

In his garden every man may be his own artist without apology or explanation. Here is one spot where each may experience the "romance of possibility."

—*Louise Beebe Wilder*

Ragbag or Quilt?

I have always regarded my home as my personal retreat. After twenty-seven years of marriage to the same man, I am truly blessed with a beautiful home life. I guess you would say that my taste has always leaned toward the more "tailored" side. As everyone was swooning over swags of English chintz and collecting wonderful antique clutter, I was busy clearing off the counters and editing the magazine basket. I was more into cacti than full-blown cabbage roses. There was no such thing as cozy clutter in my book; that was all just mess. Deep down, I equated the haphazard with lack of control. Apparently, my philosophy also applied to the great outdoors.

In our relationship, the house has been my domain, but the garden—well, that is Tom's haven. Every year he putters, pokes, and pores over a sloping stretch of garden off the back of the house. Sheltered by trees from the blaring Ohio sun, guests have always commented on Tom's glorious garden. The truth is, I never shared their enthusiasm. It was messy. It was random. It didn't look the way I envisioned. Even though I clipped pictures of pruned and manicured borders from the latest home and garden books, Tom absorbed none of my advice. He never criticized any decisions I made about how the inside of the house looked, but I wanted him to listen to me about the garden. This year was the last straw. After years of nurturing perennials and evenings of dusk-lit weeding, the garden seemed to have taken on a life of its own. Where was the plan? Where was the focus? Where was it going? I couldn't tell you what was out there, but it all had to go. Sharing my frustration with a friend who happens to be of the English let-it-be-school of gardening, she had a very different perspective.

The garden, she told me, was Tom's family. The plants were his children. He had coaxed and encouraged those "weeds" through everything. How could I consider the rototiller? I couldn't distinguish between moonbeam coreopsis and painted daisies, but Tom knew every plant by name. Where I saw weeds, he saw personalities. Where I saw a ragbag of color, he saw a complex quilt of many colors. Where I saw chaos, he looked deeper and saw a subtler order. I was so busy trying to control nature, I had missed one of the garden's greatest lessons.

Now when I look out on his riot of swaying yellow rudebeckia, I don't see weeds. I see extraordinary in the ordinary.

Sharon L. Hetzel

One of the worst mistakes you can make as a gardener
is to think you're in charge.

—*Janet Gillespie*

A Tulip for a Teacher

In 1969, I moved from an area where nothing grew except children to a quiet street with well-kept homes, freshly cut lawns, and beautiful flower beds. I purchased a two-family home and moved into the upstairs apartment. My mother and sister moved in downstairs, a nearly perfect arrangement for a family that depended on each other. It was early June and my first order of business was to make sure the yard was well maintained. My younger sister, Jean, who is the smart one in the family, walked out of the house and asked me, "Why are you watering those weeds?" Without answering, I turned off the water, rolled up the hose, and went inside the house.

Ten months later, undeterred, I was outside pulling up weeds when Jean walked out of the house and asked, "Why are you pulling those tulip bulbs out of the ground?" Dumbfounded, I responded, "But last year in this very same spot you told me these were weeds." With a mixed look of sympathy and disgust, she replied, "Tulips are spring flowers that had bloomed and withered by the time we moved in last year." I looked into the garbage can that was half filled with tulip bulbs, gave up gardening for life, and went back into the house.

Working in unusual harmony, the unsightly weeds and the beautiful tulips taught me a lesson I will never forget. The lesson is that in life there is very little that we can do alone. As smart as we might think we are, we must rely on other positive and well-meaning people to reach our goals. I'm still not a gardener, but every time I think of that half can of perfectly good tulip bulbs on their way to the city dump, I am reminded of the tragedy of a closed mind and heart, and the awesome power of positive association.

Henry Ford

In the Victorian language of flowers, tulips have special meanings. A red tulip is a declaration of love and a yellow tulip means hopeless love.

How could such sweet and wholesome hours be reckoned but in herbs and flowers?

—*Andrew Marvell*

Phoney Flowers

I went through a phase when I was constantly pressing flowers. My young son, Lantz, and I would stroll along country roadsides picking and plucking until we had gathered a basket or bag full of wildflowers. Then we would dash home and begin filling the dozen or so thick phone books that I kept around just for this purpose.

On Mother's Day, when we went to visit Grandma, we took along a handful of fresh-cut flowers for her to enjoy. When Lantz presented them to her, she exclaimed, "Oh dear! What shall I put them in?"

My son quite matter-of-factly answered, "In the phone book, Grandma!"

Celeste Lilly-Rossman

Pressing is a simple way to preserve many flowers and leaves. Be sure the plant material is dry; flowers that contain moisture will not hold their color when pressed. Use only undamaged flowers and leaves. Pick flowers at different stages of development. Press the same kind of materials in the same layer. Flowers with a thick, heavy center do not work as well as those that are flatter. Cut the flower stem close to the head. Place a layer of absorbent paper towels with no weave or embossing on a flat surface and position the leaves and flowers on top. Cover with another layer of absorbent paper towels. Place a heavy object such as a dictionary or encyclopedia on top to keep the materials flat and smooth. Allow to dry for several weeks. After drying, the flowers can be stored flat in a shoe box with layers of absorbent paper placed between each layer of flowers. Pressed flowers can be placed in a grouping and framed. They can also be used when making stationery or decorating other flat surfaces like bookmarks and journal covers. To apply, simply spread the entire surface with a thin white glue, put the flowers in a pleasing grouping, and cover over the flowers with another layer of thin white glue.

A thing of beauty is a joy forever.

—*John Keats*

Mom's Special-Delivery Rose

The birth of her daughter was nearly fatal for both her and her newborn baby. The next few days were critical. The trauma on the now-weakened mother had resulted in blindness. The doctors were not certain whether her vision would be restored.

The baby girl who was being closely monitored in the ICU had suffered massive bruising from the effect of the instruments that were necessary to force her from her mother's narrow womb. The father was never far away from either of his "girls," praying for their very lives. The dozen red roses that he brought to signify celebration sat unnoticed on the hospital nightstand, patiently waiting for the appreciative smile of his wife.

It seemed like a lifetime, but on the fourth day, the father's prayers were finally answered. His wife, the mother of his child, was slowly regaining her sight. As her vision improved, she longed to see her new baby. She and her husband had long since decided to call the child Marilyn if it was a girl. "Bring in Marilyn," she pleaded. Baby Marilyn's condition had improved enough for her to be placed in the loving arms of her mother. The anticipation of the awaited moment could be seen in the mother's strained eyes. The precious moment arrived, and as she gazed upon the disfigured features of her baby, tears welled in her eyes. "Oh, Marilyn, my baby," she sobbed and held her closer.

The attending nurse felt the mother's deep disappointment and despair over the appearance of the tiny baby. As she tried to find the words of comfort that would encourage her, she noticed the beautiful roses on the bedside table and suggested calling the baby Rose in the hope that the baby would grow to be as beautiful as a rose.

As her tears slowed, the mother gradually began to focus on her surroundings. She looked at the beautiful arrangement of roses. The gift from her husband once meant to congratulate now served to inspire. "I will call her Rose," the mother declared. "And someday she will grow to be as beautiful as this symbol of our love."

The parents in this story are mine, and through their encouragement I have blossomed by becoming a floral designer. Daily, as I create flower arrangements for my customers, I often think of the many symbolic meanings of the rose and try to use those meanings as my inspiration.

Marilyn Rose Brosang

TO BRIGHTEN OUR DARKEST HOURS

5.

FLOWERS LEAVE SOME OF THEIR FRAGRANCE IN THE HAND THAT BESTOWS THEM.

—*Chinese proverb*

An Eternal Rose

My father grew roses. Not just a few bushes for color in the landscaping, but whole gardens of them. I remember roses galore from when I was a little girl; and when he died at more than eighty years of age, he had at least that many bushes blooming around our home. Toward the last, he would sit in his chair directing his grandchildren, my sons, on how to dig the holes, what amount of fertilizer to throw in the bottom, how to spread the roots out, and, finally, how to gently water, prune, and love them as they grew.

He was a hard-working man who spent years, from age thirteen till well into his seventies, toiling in factories. But he knew the value of having beauty just for beauty's sake. How he loved to pick the best ones to give to those who especially needed them—friends, relatives, coworkers.

On the day of his funeral, my sons slipped out of the house before the hearse arrived. I did not know why until I saw them go to his casket for the last time, each with a rose in hand—to place in his. So my father holds forever that which brought him and so many others pleasure during his lifetime. Roses.

Later that day as I sat alone, one of my sons came to hand me the rose he had worn in his lapel. He said, "Here, Mom. I thought you would want this." And I saw my father once again.

Lois DiGiacomo

Flowers for a Princess

In life, she was known to enjoy sending flowers. In death, she was showered with them as the streets outside London's palaces turned into fields of flowers. England—and the world—mourned the tragic death of Diana, Princess of Wales, with some 60 million stems. People reached out to touch a legend and made a bit of history. When news of her death was announced, it stunned the entire world into silence. No words could begin to express the emotion felt by people everywhere and in every station of life. The only "language" powerful enough to convey the vastness of their love and sympathy was the language of flowers. The only way they knew to comfort themselves and to share in the communal grieving was with flowers.

During the days following Diana's death, the demand for flowers was enormous, as was the work of those who labored behind the scenes to make this outpouring possible. It is completely mind-boggling to conceive of the logistics necessary to prepare the flowers for an event of this magnitude. To those who labored so tirelessly at a time when they, too, were grieving, we owe an immense debt of gratitude.

Overwhelmingly people requested lilies, as it was known that lilies, specifically *longiflorum* (Madonna) lilies, were Diana's favorite flower. Other white flowers, such as roses and freesia, were also popular because they are traditional funeral flowers and stand for purity, a fitting symbol for a princess who died young, at thirty-six.

By official count, more than one and a half million bouquets were stacked outside the royal palaces by the time of the funeral. So dense were the floral offerings that they were visible from an airplane flying five thousand feet above the city of London. At Buckingham Palace there was such an avalanche of arrangements to deal with that, toward the end, the palace requested that people combine their individual bouquets and message cards into larger, collective bouquets. With the flowers surrounding Kensington Palace at waist level, a team began clearing away the estimated ten to fifteen thousand tons of flowers that blanketed the city. Countless volunteers, including Boy Scouts and Girl Scouts, joined the groundskeepers to scoop up the offerings. Flowers that were still fresh were taken to hospitals and hospices. The 90 percent that had faded were taken to Kensington Gardens leaf yard, to be composted for use in Kensington Garden and other royal parks.

Not only were flowers piled high at the gates, but they were tossed in vast numbers onto the passing funeral bier, a sad reminder of Diana's wedding day, when the princess's path was also strewn with flowers. Yet, in a very real sense, Diana's funeral was a celebration as well—a celebration of her life and of what she had done for others.

Diana had been in the public eye for years, and the image of her most of us will remember is of the beautiful princess carrying a bouquet of flowers. Whether she was garbed in the finest ball gown or the most casual dress, flowers seemed to be her perfect accessory, more becoming and better suited to her than any crown jewels could ever be. I can't remember anyone in modern history who in such a short lifetime received as many flowers as Princess Diana, and how warmly and graciously she accepted them!

In life and in death, the flowers Diana received as gifts were symbolic of the love people felt for her, an expression of their appreciation for her compassion and her ability to touch them—physically and emotionally. Diana's compassion was legendary. A lonely child, and later a lonely adult, who knew the sting of rejection, she was quick to extend her hand to the weak and the wounded. In the early '80s, when those stricken by AIDS were made to feel like outcasts, she was among the first to reach out to them with love and understanding and set an example for the rest of the world.

In death, the floral tributes to the princess also signified "We'll miss you." Diana touched people all over the world, across the seas and across the classes, and the flowers that arrived to memorialize her came from ordinary folks as well as from the inhabitants of palaces and prisons. Few women—indeed, few people—in history have had her ability to relate across all boundaries. Flowers were the international language for the family of man that mourned her loss.

Our deepest sympathy goes out to Diana's family, who will personally mourn this beautiful English rose, and all those the world over who will miss the twinkle in her eyes, her radiant smile, her sweet embrace, and her acts of kindness. It's comforting to know that her memory and her mission will live on.

Rocky Pollitz

The rose is the flower of love and the most popular flower ever grown. Nebuchadnezzar used them to decorate his palace. In Persia they were grown for their perfume oil, and the sultan filled his mattress with the petals. They have been strewn in the river to welcome heroes and later became synonymous with the worst excesses of the Roman Empire. Royalty filled their swimming baths and fountains with rosewater and sat on carpets of rose petals for their feasts.

Nature does not know extinction; all it knows is transformation. Everything science has taught me, and continues to teach me, strengthens my belief in the continuity of our spiritual existence after death.

—*Werner von Braun*

Bittersweet Beauty

I stood in the courtyard facing a small gathering of friends, family, caregivers, and acquaintances. For many, it was the first time they'd met each other. For all of us, we shared a common thread—my mother. Her planter boxes, blooming with sunflowers and nasturtiums, sighed in the intense heat of the afternoon. Looking up past the apartment windows that surrounded the courtyard and framed a piece of the Seattle skyline, I noted a seagull gliding across the blue sky.

Bringing my attention back to the people seated in front of me, I thought about my mother, who had suffered so many ups and downs but who also taught me much and introduced me to the joys of gardening and the world of plants. . . .

As a mother of five, she had little time during the day to be out in the garden tending to the flowers or transplanting shrubs, but as soon as we were tucked away in bed, she'd grab her hand tools and car keys and go outside into the night. Starting up the car, Mom would move it into position so the headlights could shine on a section of the garden. Peaceful and quiet at last, she'd settle into a gentle rhythm of weeding.

When we were older, all of us participated in yard chores, and some were not so pleasant. Slugs, for example, were attacked with slug bait and salt. Mom "detested" slugs (she also detested the word "hate"). Slugs chomped on her daffodils, defoliated seedlings, and maimed her budding rhododendrons. Handing out salt shakers, she ushered us out the door with instructions to seek out and salt the enemy. Years later, we were still finding salt shakers strewn around the property like weapons on a battlefield.

When we headed out for one of our family hiking trips, I'd look for unusual plants, ones I didn't think Mom would recognize. I would proudly present her with a sample of every oddball flora I found. Thus challenged, she'd open her wild plants guide, and together we'd flip through the chapters, looking for a match. When I was much older, I came across the battered book and discovered dried leaves and flowers pressed between its pages.

During my senior year in high school, I took a forestry course, never imagining that my mom's love of plants would get me out of a final exam. The student who brought in and correctly identified the greatest number of native plants was exempt from the big test. The night before class, Mom and I toured the yard collecting samples that we labeled and packed in a cardboard box. The next day I (we) won, hands down!

As the years went by, Mom and Dad divorced and Mom struggled with increasing alcoholism and mental illness. Unable to hold a job for long, she ended up in low-income housing, a block from Seattle's Pike Place Market. Undaunted by being in the middle of the city, she was determined to be near greenery and plants, so each spring and summer she rode the bus to and from her community plot.

During the worst of her years, Mom withdrew from us, making normal communication uneasy, at times impossible. But in her last year, after being diagnosed with terminal cancer, her mental illness left her and we could have whole conversations, walks, and meals together. Saddened by the cancer, but grateful for the change in her mental and emotional state, I made several visits to her from my home in Kodiak, Alaska.

On a mid-summer morning I was out in the garden when my older brother and sister telephoned from her room at the hospital in Washington to say that Mom was failing. Needing to be alone, I returned to my garden where I picked a bouquet of tall, yellow iris to carry to the house. The phone was ringing again. It was my sister who, holding the phone, let me talk to Mom in her last moments of consciousness. I spoke the words that I had never spoken before. I told her how my garden always reminded me of her, how grateful I was for all she had taught me, how much I loved her. My mother died that evening.

The following morning, while trying to prepare for my trip to Seattle, I came across a box of family papers and photographs. Inside I found a Japanese print Mom and I had selected together over twenty years before. It was a beautiful garden scene. In the foreground was a clump of yellow irises.

Now, I squinted in the afternoon sun and collected my thoughts for the audience in the courtyard. "I'm happy that Mom now knows peace and freedom from pain," I began. "And I'm grateful for her encouraging that 'just do it' attitude she instilled in me." Taking a breath, I wiped away a tear, looked up, and smiled, "But I must say I'm a little jealous of where she is right now, because in heaven, there are no slugs."

Marion Stirrup Owen

The iris was a favorite flower of royalty, including the kings of France who used it as inspiration for their royal emblem and called it the fleur-de-lys. In Greek mythology, Iris was the messenger of the Greek gods. She appeared to mortals in the form of a rainbow. There are as many colors of iris as there are colors in the rainbow.

Love's language may be talked with these;
To work out choicest sentences
No blossoms can be meeter;
And, such being used in Eastern bowers,
Young maids may wonder if the flowers
Or meanings be the sweeter.

—Elizabeth Barrett Browning

The Language of Flowers

The Victorian language of flowers, which is not often remembered, proved indispensable when I really needed it. In the language of flowers, each flower and herb represents, or symbolizes, a sentiment. Familiar examples of the flower language that everyone knows include the red rose for love, the olive branch for peace, and the mighty oak for strength. Now imagine a thousand sentiments represented by flowers, herbs, grasses, ferns, vines, shrubs, and trees instead of by words, and you will know what is meant by the Language of Flowers.

For a number of years, my dear friends had hoped for a baby to complete their family, and after concern about whether or not they were too old, they were finally expecting. With obvious joy, my friend ate sensibly, exercised in moderation, visited the doctor, decorated the nursery—did all the right things. But the way of God is not always clear to us. When the blessed event was only three months away, in a devastating, wrenching loss, she miscarried.

She wept inconsolably for the child she would never know. She didn't want to hear that she could have another baby—she wanted that particular baby. I didn't know what to say; I felt awkward talking about her loss, and worse still keeping silent. It was then that I decided to literally "say it with flowers."

With great care, I gathered just the right flowers and herbs from my garden to do my talking for me, and assembled them into a formal little bouquet. Such a talking bouquet is called a "tussie-mussie," and it is assembled by selecting flowers and leaves based on their symbolism as well as their beauty. After choosing the plants that expressed the feelings I felt too shy to say, I wrote a card for her listing the plants and their sentiments. In this way I was able to acknowledge her grief and express my support without embarrassing both of us.

I included a white rosebud for *a heart untouched by love* and grasses for *the fleeting quality of life*. Marigolds represented *grief,* wood sorrel symbolized *maternal love,* and elderberry stood for *sympathy and kindness*. To finish, I added goldenrod for *encouragement,* stonecrop for *tranquillity,* and flowering reed for *confidence in heaven*. I tied the tussie-mussie with satiny ribbons, and delivered it, along with the explanatory card, with love and affection. The Victorian Language of Flowers came to the rescue and helped me to convey my feelings, ease my friend's grief, and strengthen our friendship. Try speaking the Language of Flowers the next time you're searching for just the right words.

Geraldine Adamich Laufer

Although most gardeners don't go into gardening with the object of improving themselves, shy people become friendly and stiff ones thaw out, and the most unsuspected talents for combining colors both indoors and out are manifested.

—Helen Morgenthau Fox

The Rest of My Life

My passion for flowers began at a very early age, instilled in me by my mother, who has always had glorious cutting gardens over the years. When I was a child of five, we even moved to Lilac Lane, where I had the aroma of those beautiful flowers to help lull me to sleep on spring nights. But the final significance of flowers came to me by assessing a personal tragedy.

In August 1988, I received shocking news that would control my life for years to come. My husband, Jeff, had been hospitalized for what we thought was pneumonia. When his condition didn't improve with antibiotics, the doctor admitted him to UC Medical Center in San Francisco for further tests. For our third anniversary, which occurred just as he was hospitalized, I brought him a basket of flowers to lift his spirits. On my way to his room, I passed the doctor who had conducted the broncoscopy. "Mrs. LaForce," he said, "we have the test results back. Your husband has terminal lung cancer. He has less than six months to live." This was certainly not the anniversary we had planned, not the life we'd hoped for.

Over the next seven months, through radiation and chemotherapy, Jeff was very brave, but the only thing that cheered him were the floral bouquets I regularly brought home or to the hospital. He always focused on their beauty and enjoyed their smell.

Late in March 1989, Jeff decided to give up his fight. We had a long talk and one of the last things he said to me was, "I love you with all of my heart, and I want you to do something you love for the rest of your life. Bring joy to your life and those of others, for life is too short."

Two years later, I decided to pursue floral design as a hobby at the local college, eventually starting a part-time floral design business specializing in freeze-drying flowers. In 1994, I was able to leave my corporate job for full-time entrepreneurship. Today, I preserve hundreds of special occasion flowers for people from all walks of life. Those flowers are memories of wedding days, christenings, proms, and sometimes memorials for a dear loved one who has passed.

The lesson I learned through this experience is that life is short and we should enjoy each moment of it through the beauty offered to us. Take the time to smell the rose. Enjoy the sunflower smiling at you. Through these you will be reminded of how precious our lives are, in both happy and sad times, and how each person we love during our lifetime helps us to grow and molds us into the person we become.

Kathie LaForce

The Italian name for the sunflower is *girasole,* from the Italian *girare,* to turn, and *sole,* sun, because this garden flower turns its head to follow the sun as it travels from east to west.

A garden is a place to feel the beauty of solitude.

—*Bob Barnes*

In Full Bloom with Him

My daughter Suzan's favorite flower was the gardenia. We had two gardenia bushes at our home—one in the front yard, one in the back. The one in the backyard had blossomed very normally, and the one in the front, although several years old, had never bloomed. Suzan passed away on May 13, 1995. About three weeks later, returning from a trip, we noticed that the bush in the front yard had a few blooms, and the one in the backyard was inundated with blossoms—much earlier than usual—and was absolutely beautiful. It seemed to us that God was reminding us that Suzan is in "full bloom" with Him. The gardenia, needless to say, is now one of my favorites.

Zig Ziglar

Flowers Deliver

My sister moved to Hawaii when her new husband wanted to return to his native home. They had met while he was stationed in Ohio as a U.S. agricultural agent. We became letter writers and package senders. Members of the family visited my sister for great family vacations. As the years went by, my sister experienced many of the same problems my mother had had in maintaining a pregnancy. Finally, after several attempts, she was almost completely full term, and the entire family was terribly excited, both in Hawaii and in Ohio.

Having been a florist for many years, I knew firsthand how important flowers could be at certain times in our lives. I had helped with the joy weddings celebrate, the surprise birthday flowers can bring, and the happiness and satisfaction anniversary flowers provide.

When the news came that she had delivered a stillborn baby, we were beside ourselves with grief. A close family, we knew that even if we boarded a plane immediately, no one could be with her for many, many hours.

But we knew that flowers could be delivered. It was only a matter of minutes before a custom-made, beautiful floral arrangement was delivered to her, complete with a personalized card. When we just couldn't arrive fast enough, when we had to communicate to my beloved sister our thoughts and prayers, flowers got through.

Today, my sister is the proud mother of two grown children. In addition to letters and packages, we often send flowers, sometimes for special occasions, sometimes "just because." But of all the flowers or gifts we have sent, none is more emotional than the bouquet of flowers that reached my sister faster than we could at a time when we all needed the comfort of each other. At that point the "hug" of flowers was the best hug we could provide.

Alan K. Parkhurst

One day, on a very busy street in San Francisco, I was lost in my own thoughts on my way to a presentation.

Suddenly, an intoxicating aroma broke through the existing city smells and stopped me in my tracks. I turned and looked around . . . and then I saw them—the gardenias in the flower vendor's hut. The one I purchased scented the room where I spoke that afternoon, and its scent kept me company that night in the hotel as it floated in a bowl of water next to my bed. I wonder what the maid thought the next day when she found it—still floating, still lovely—filling the room with fragrance.

Every gardener knows that under the cloak of winter
lies a miracle . . . a seed waiting to sprout,
a bulb opening to the light, a bud straining to unfurl.
And the anticipation nurtures our dream.

—*Barbara Winkler*

The Miracle of the Magnolia Tree

One year, my husband, Pat, and I planted a very small magnolia tree outside our bedroom window. We watched it grow and gave it much loving care. Several years went by while we watched for the much-anticipated blossoms, but the tree was still too young; the springs came and went and we didn't spot a single bud or blossom. We could hardly wait to be cheered by the lovely flowers. Pat had been battling multiple sclerosis and the disease was gaining ground. Spring came again, and as we looked out to view our tree, there it was—a breathtakingly large waxy magnolia blossom, but oddly enough, only one, blooming on the side of the tree closest to our window. We were incredibly gratified by the sight, and though Pat was quite ill and weak, the beautiful flower gave him such joy! He passed away that spring, and every time I see a magnolia tree in bloom I think of the miracle of our magnolia tree.

Betty Valle

While with an eye made quiet by the power,
Of harmony and the deep power of joy,
We see into the life of things.

— *William Wordsworth*

A Gift from My Brother

My family always enjoyed taking strolls through the woods. We often collected native flora and would sometimes dry these keepsakes for later use. I once asked my brother, who liked to call me "flower girl," if he minded us gathering a few things from his yard. As we ventured off, he teased, "I've got more *weeds* than roses!"

Truthfully, I didn't know he had *any* roses. His bachelor pad was not exactly landscaped, but his rose comment sparked my curiosity; and sure enough we found them, a huge old shrub of miniature pink blossoms.

I picked several handfuls and took them home to dry. Later I strung the tiny heads into a necklace. I had no real intention of ever wearing it. I only thought it would look pretty lying on the dresser.

Just a few short weeks later, my brother was killed in an auto accident. As I was leaving my house on the heartbreaking day of his funeral, I went to my dresser, picked up the rose necklace, and carefully put it on.

Inevitably, many of the friends and family who attended the service commented on my unusual necklace. At a time when words were few, the small blossoms gave way to healing conversation. Sometimes the smallest "gift" can leave the biggest impression.

Celeste Lilly-Rossman

Air-drying allows moisture in plant materials to evaporate naturally. Simply bunch like materials, such as a bouquet of roses, together in small clusters, tie them with rubber bands or string, and hang them upside down in a dark, dry, warm place.

The exceeding beauty of the earth
in her splendor yields
a new thought with every petal.

—*Richard Jeffries*

Dad's Christmas Cactus

I was living in Colorado and my folks had come out from Illinois to visit. Although I'm rarely ill, a nasty flu decided to pay me a visit at the same time as my parents. My mom took over the cooking and other chores, and my dad bought books on subjects that interested me. They both wrapped me with tender, loving care, making me feel as protected and secure as I had as a child. One day, Dad brought home a little Christmas cactus with its cheery red flowers. He balanced the plant on my chest, as if close contact with those bright blooms would infuse me with renewed zest.

I'm not known for my green thumb, yet for years that cactus bloomed, once in the summer and again at Christmastime. The blossoms never failed to cheer me or remind me of the love and care of my parents.

In November of 1987, with all five of his children and his wife at his side, Dad passed away. Afterward, I returned home to Colorado and set about the task of watering my flowers, which had grown dry in my absence. When I came to my Christmas cactus, it was in full bloom—more than a month ahead of schedule and with more blossoms than ever before. I was so stunned at this show of beauty that I stopped my watering and just stood staring at it. At that moment, I felt my father's presence. A warmth, as if I'd been wrapped in a warm blanket, flooded over me. Somehow, I knew he was smiling. Every year since then, my Christmas cactus has been in full bloom on the anniversary of Dad's death. It is a reminder of warmth and security—the care and love of my dad.

Dona Abbott

Form a bunch of one hundred or more fresh lavender stems, keeping the flower heads even. Tie together securely halfway between the flowers and the ends of the stems. Cut the stems so that they are perfectly even at the bottom of the bunch; the bunch will now stand by itself. As a finishing touch, tie a pretty ribbon around it.

To pick a flower is so much more satisfying than just observing it, or photographing it. . . . So in later years I have grown in my garden as many flowers as possible for children to pick.

Anne Scott-James

Bruno's Roses

It was just a rosebush, more wild than cultivated. Not quite red, but something more than pink. It grew at the end of my grandfather's garden.

Apparently he had planned to become a printer, but the Great Depression got in the way. When he found work, it was as a machine operator with International Harvester in Milwaukee. It was steady work for a man who knew what it was to want, so he stayed, working in the factory right on through the war and into the mid-1950s. He was there long enough to know he could someday count on the company's modest pension. When "someday" arrived, he packed up his family and bought a little country store and tavern about an hour's drive northwest of the city.

I came along about ten years later, in the middle of my grandfather's second career. My earliest memories are of him sweeping up, washing glasses, moving cases of empty bottles and struggling with barrels of beer. He was gruff with his customers, quick to cuss, and rarely gave anyone a drink on the house. Even his name, Bruno, bespoke hard work and toughness. But Grampa Bruno was still likable and always had time to smile and joke with me. But if I asked him to take a walk down by the lake or up over the hill, he would remind me that there was work to be done. It seemed that all he did was work.

Then, when I turned ten, he retired again, first to a little house by a river. But he wanted more space and bought the first twenty-acre farmette he saw for sale. The yard at this farm was dotted with thorny treasures, but it was the rosebush at the end of the garden that seemed to get most of Bruno's attention. He would carefully prune it, check its leaves and stems for any disease or infestation, and remind me every time I touched the lawn mower to "be damn careful around the rosebush."

That farm and my grandfather's gruff guidance—he had an opinion on *everything*—became my sanctuary through a tumultuous adolescence. Those years were punctuated by my parents' divorce and my brother's battle with drugs, but what I remember most is listening to a man who surprised everyone when he talked about his rosebush. Who would have guessed Bruno liked roses?

A few years later I came home on leave from the navy to find the rosebush badly in need of care.

"I'm just getting too damned old," growled Bruno when I asked him about the bush. He then provided plenty of direction and a careful eye as I clipped here and there to thin the bush.

"That should do it," he said, grabbing my shoulder as I reached to make one more cut. "The damned thing will probably live longer than me."

Three weeks later and back on duty, a chief petty officer came to tell me that my grandfather had died of heart failure while working in the garden. My only input for the funeral service was a request that roses be printed on the front of the prayer card.

As we laid him to rest, I vowed to find my own "rosebush" long before I ever retired.

Kevin Michalowski

When you're planning your garden, keep in mind how it looks in different kinds of light, at different times of the day. In the morning, the light is pale pink, in the afternoon, clear and bright. Just before a massive thunderstorm the light is purplish. The kind of light under which we view a garden directly affects our perception of the garden and the impact the garden colors have made in our minds.

In all the recipes for happiness I have ever seen,
"something to look forward to" has been given as
an important ingredient. Something to look forward to!
How rich the gardener, any gardener, is in this particular
integrant! For always he looks forward to something
if it is only the appearance of the red noses of the Peonies
in the spring or the sharp aromas that fill the air in
autumn after the frost has touched the herbage.

—*Louise Beebe Wilder*

Rebirth

My best friend's mother, Nancy, loved the simple things in life: family, friends, God, and flowers. Among those flowers she loved most was her simple yet elegant *spathiphyllum,* or peace lily. It was always beautiful, almost always in bloom. She was a pro.

On a warm, sunny day in May, God took Nancy from her place on earth. No warnings, no questions asked. All those close to her clung to her belongings, anything and everything to keep her memory alive. The *spathiphyllum* was in high demand. To no avail, however, since the prized beauty would never be as spectacular as it had been in her care. No one knew her secrets. All hope lost, the withered plant was carried to the basement.

When spring-cleaning time came two years later, we found the *spathiphyllum.* Its crinkled, brown foliage covered the container. The soil was so dry it pulled away from the sides of the pot. Not a glimpse of green was to be seen. The prized *spathiphyllum* was dead.

Container and all was placed outside, forgotten, on its way to the garbage. But it seems Nancy didn't—from up above, she had her eye on that beloved peace lily. Right before the garbage trucks arrived to cart the sorry *spathiphyllum* off to the dump, we noticed a budding bit of greenery. It was alive once again, preparing to bloom in this new time, with this new life, simple yet elegant—just like Nancy, who is now surrounded by all the flowers she could ever want.

Sara Rowekamp

Pollen is commonly found on the anthers in the center of lilies. If this pollen rubs off onto clothing or fabrics, it stains. Try brushing the pollen away with a chenille stem or pipe cleaner. You can also leave the garment out in the hot sun to let the lily pollen oils dry up. Shake the cloth and the pollen will fall off. To keep this from happening, simply remove the pollen prior to using or displaying the lilies. This is easily done by pulling the pollen pods off the anthers. Be sure to wash your hands well afterward.

It's no secret that growing things soothe the mind,
that wild things uplift the soul, that rocks
and hills and trees do something undefinable but
positive for the human spirit.

—Thomas Kinkade

Floratherapy

All over the world, nature has been the source of inspiration for artists. It has also provided physicians with an integral source of healing in its plants and flowers. But I have found that a single cut flower has the power to heal a person.

I was born in Viet Nam, and since I was a bright child it was planned that I would study the sciences or medicine. At the time,

I was also passionately interested in flowers—their colors, shapes, and scents. When I got older, I went to school in Japan where I began studying medicine, but finances required that I switch to chemical engineering because of a scholarship available to me.

At that time, my aunt was seriously ill and I often brought flowers to her in the hospital. She was surrounded by patients who were equally ill, and I noticed the contrast between the lovely flowers and the misery of those who were so sick. The idea came to me that I could bring together all of my passions—my love for flowers, my feelings about medicine, and my desire to heal. When I was completing my university degree in chemistry in Japan, I spent all of my spare time taking Japanese floral art courses. This hobby has become a twenty-year passion; and together with my study of psychology, traditional Chinese medicine, acupuncture, and naturotherapy, I feel I have established direct links among universal laws, natural laws, and the health of a person.

I have developed a therapy using flowers. It involves people making flower arrangements and then, with my assistance, analyzing or decoding their arrangements so that they may better understand their inner worlds and improve their organizational skills in all aspects of their lives. Because flowers have a calming effect on people, my clients learn in a gentle, nonthreatening environment.

I employ basic principles from my studies and my Asian heritage in the floratherapy I practice and teach. Most Oriental philosophies are concerned with the parallels between the universe and man and the balance between the two. At first my clients create flower arrangements and I analyze them. Then I teach them to analyze their own creations so that they may explore the ways in which they are balancing their inner and outer worlds. Yang and yin are also important principles to understand. The yang, the element of height, possesses the male traits of solar energy. It is positive, radiating, and reflects the external. The yin, the element of depth, possesses the female traits of lunar energy. Its energy is negative and absorbing, reflecting the internal.

I also use the techniques of Ikebana, the Japanese floral art that reproduces, in miniature, the universe by representing heaven, earth, and man. Ikebana works with the positioning of each element, its depth and balance, and the proportions among items. The highest positioned floral element, "heaven," is placed at the back of the arrangement, representing that element which corresponds to life on earth through the sun and the rain. The lowest positioned floral element, "earth," is placed at the front, representing the mother who gives life, nurtures, and develops all living things. Positioned in the middle, "man" is situated between heaven and earth. Man represents the intelligent being who, as the closest to God, runs and balances life on earth. The placement of people's elements in their arrangements helps them to understand, and even change, themselves.

I also draw upon Zen philosophy. According to Zen, man is able to find inner harmony when he is in harmony with nature, so the execution of a floral arrangement is done in silence and reflection. By concentrating on the manipulation of the flowers—their form, color, and beauty—people establish a harmonious relationship between themselves and their universe. The entire creative process allows them to find the desired tranquillity to regain the equilibrium needed to heal.

A final aspect is color analysis, because color choice reflects personality traits, emotions, and situations, and allows people to identify themselves. For example, yellow is a hot, masculine color radiating energy. People suffering from depression rarely use yellow in a design. In floratherapy, the expression of emotions is an integral part of the therapeutic process.

The role of the floratherapist is to help clients observe and analyze their floral arrangement and establish the links between the components and their lives. People learn to liberate themselves from suffering. This ongoing process promotes growth and the integration of stability.

Like the artists and physicians who have been creatively and practically inspired by nature, I, too, have recognized its power and beauty. It has given me its many beautiful plants and flowers to help liberate people from suffering, to help them heal themselves.

Nguyen Ngoc Lan

Feeling depressed? Don't walk into a room filled with dark colors that have little connection with the outdoors. Change the atmosphere of your environment and go outside for a walk or take off your shoes and walk through the grass in the park. A garden filled with colorful blossoms is also a perfect place to get some relief from the blues.

It is good to be alone in a garden at dawn or
dark so that all its shy presences may haunt you and
possess you in a reverie of suspended thought.

—James Douglas

Planting Hope

In 1992, I was going through a horrible depression. I was so far down that to hit bottom I would have needed to jump up.

For years I had been successful and productive, but now I felt as though I was so paralyzed by my depression that I could not move forward. Then I remembered a quote I had read somewhere: "Even if I knew the world would come to an end tomorrow, I would still plant my flowers today." So, on one of the worst days, I ventured out of my house, at the time, my security blanket, and drove to the store to get some bedding plants. All the way there and back home, I cried. Part of me wanted nothing to do with these plants and I didn't know exactly what to do with them, but in my fragile emotional state, for some reason I was compelled to buy them and bring them home.

Since my energy level was almost nonexistent, all I wanted to do was curl up in bed and sleep, but I forced myself to go outside and plant a bunch of the young flowers in front of my house. It was painstaking work, and at the time I thought it was useless, but I did the planting to keep my mind off the depression and just to do something.

I had become so used to seeing the world in shades of gray that one week later, as I was coming home in my usual sad state, I suddenly noticed that my little bedding plants had miraculously turned into gorgeous flowers. I'd practically forgotten about them after I'd put them in the ground, but now they were growing like crazy. Tears of joy—not unexplained tears now—filled my eyes, and hope filled my weakened soul as I saw progress in my gardening project, the first real progress I'd made in a long time. Though Mother Nature had lent a hand, I took pride in what I'd done and saw these budding flowers as a sign of hope—and a first real step toward breaking the cycle of depression that had gripped me for so long. As I regained my foothold in life, I drew strength and courage from my little garden, and I remembered again how true was the phrase "Even if I knew the world would come to an end tomorrow, I would still plant my flowers today."

Peter V. Cannice

Thou art the Iris, fair among the fairest,
Who, armed with golden rod
And winged with the celestial azure, bearest
The message of some God.

—Henry Wadsworth Longfellow

A Single White Rose

Tragic events can change our lives in an instant. Yet, if we are fortunate, human kindness, even in the simple form of flowers, can lessen our pain. Such has been the case in our family.

I had grown up in a small town where families were the center of lives. Loving dolls and baby-sitting, I could hardly wait to be a mother. After college, a brief teaching career, and marriage to a wonderful man named Charlie, I did just that. We celebrated the birth of our first son, Garrett, and life was beautiful.

For several more years it continued that way. We bought our small English cottage, Charlie was doing well at work, Garrett was thriving, and I was again pregnant. Our lives were busy, fulfilling and normal, and our second son, Gavin Ward Glanz, was born with only the slight problem of being two and a half weeks early. We spent the evening of his birth phoning family and friends so they could share our joy, but the next day the nightmare began.

When our pediatrician, a personal friend, walked into my room early the next morning, I immediately knew something was wrong. With great difficulty, he told us that he thought our baby son had a congenital heart defect, and so he was taken to Cook County Children's Hospital, to the best pediatric cardiologist in the area. He encouraged us not to give up hope, because open-heart surgery could be performed. While Charlie followed the ambulance, I began the awful waiting. Later that afternoon, Charlie called to tell me that our baby had died. The problem turned out to be with his lungs, and there was no way to save him. He was buried on Christmas Eve.

I know that never again in my life will I feel so helpless and so completely empty. Because none of our family or friends ever got to know him, hold him, or even see his picture, since the hospital didn't take one, they had a difficult time relating to our grief; and although they were sad for us, they really felt little connection to our son. As a result, much of the time Charlie and I felt alone in our deep love for him and in the terrible loss of not being able to watch him grow and become an adult.

I tried to pick up the pieces of my life, especially since we had a young son who needed me; however, there were days when I didn't think I could even make it through the morning, so deep was my grief and my sense of loss. Eventually I learned to be fully present and to treasure every minute of every day, but I still struggled with people's reluctance to talk about our son, their lack of memories of him, and the terrible void in my life.

On the day that would have been Gavin's first birthday, the doorbell rang; there on the doorstep was a delivery man from the florist. He had a small bud vase holding one single white rose. With it was a card from some very dear friends that read, "This is in memory of a very special life, one which we know will make a difference in this world—Gavin Ward Glanz." And each year for many years on the same day, that single white rose has arrived on our doorstep as a symbol that someone in this often indifferent, rushed world of ours does remember the life of our little boy.

And they were right—he has made a difference in this world through me, the person I have become because of his life and death, and the abiding message of hope I am able to share with others as I speak all over the world.

A beautiful postscript to this story is that last year our first little grandson was born and named Gavin William Glanz. How very blessed we are! Our son lives on through this precious gift of new life, and we will always celebrate our new little Gavin's birthday with one single white rose.

Barbara Glanz

HEIRLOOM FLOWERS

6.

NO OCCUPATION IS SO DELIGHTFUL TO ME AS THE CULTURE OF THE EARTH AND NO CULTURE COMPARABLE TO THAT OF THE GARDEN.

—*Thomas Jefferson*

When the Peonies Bloom

My mother was a genius at getting flowers to grow. She could take a plant that looked nearly dead and not only coax it back to life, but seemingly convince that plant that it had a responsibility to make all who saw its blossoms recognize God's handiwork. Her yard was a rainbow palette of colors and textures. But the display that caused many people from our small town to drive down our rural lane slowly was a luxuriously thick hedge of peonies that lined our entire driveway, the rich fragrance blending into a delightful bouquet no perfume could ever equal.

Several months after Mother's death, my brother appeared at my door one day with a large box, a bag of fertilizer, and a shovel. He knew how much my sisters and I had loved our mother's gardens, and how much we had grieved over our memories of the loving attention she had given to the peony hedges, which were to be left behind when the homestead was sold. He was also wise enough to know how little of our mother's skill with growing things we had inherited. His memorial to her, and his gift to us, was to bring each of us several plants from that hedge and plant them in our yards.

Now every spring as the peonies burst into flowers, we telephone each other and marvel all over again at the legacy of love that our mother nurtured: not only in that fabulous garden, but also in her son, who made certain we would always have a beautiful, shared reminder of our wonderful mother.

Sharon McVary

The peony is a native of China, where it has been grown since the eighth century. The red peony was the most prized and was considered the king of the flowers. Its rich, dark color and bulbous shape became symbolic of abundance.

If you would have a lovely garden,
you should have a lovely life.

—*The Gardener's Manual, 1843*

Zucchini Flowers

My father was born on a mountainside in Italy. A trip to the nearest town meant a mile-long hike down the mountain and, of course, a very tiresome journey back up. Times were hard and food was scarce, so the family raised their own vegetables, selling any surplus in town to purchase other necessities. Farming the sparse land was quite difficult because the area was so rocky. The precious dirt was carefully gathered, and the mountainside was painstakingly terraced to preserve every bit of soil. To my father, the blossoms of the tomatoes, peppers, and other vegetables were beautiful, for they meant food for the family. The blossoms he loved best of all were the zucchini flowers.

My mother, on the other hand, was raised in a more prosperous family. When she married my father and went to live on the mountain, she planted carnations all around their home, much to his dismay. He considered them a waste of the painstakingly maintained soil because they could not provide nourishment for his family.

After he brought his family to America, my father always

planted a garden. His pride and joy was still the blossoms of the plants that would yield the precious vegetables his family could eat. His special love remained the zucchini flowers, which he carefully harvested early every day since they had to be picked before they opened completely and were then considered inedible. Once in full bloom, he considered them worthless. Some days, perhaps, there would be only one flower ready to harvest. It had to be picked and saved until there were enough blossoms to cook in a delicious omelet. He often shared this delicacy with friends and relatives.

My mother continued to plant the flowers she loved. While my father never objected, he would always sneak a few vegetables into her flower beds when she wasn't looking.

Today we still plant zucchini in our small garden. Always my thoughts go to my father as I find myself carefully collecting every precious blossom just as he did. When we visit his grave, we bring one of his beloved vegetable plants, preferably one with unopened blossoms on it.

Josephine Lamancusa

Zucchini blossoms make a delectable appetizer or side dish for an entrée. Pick the young zucchini with the blossoms attached. Slice them in half, then dip with the cut side down into melted butter, then cornmeal. Pan-fry in a few tablespoons of hot olive oil, over medium-high heat, for about three minutes, until lightly browned. Drain on a paper towel and serve immediately.

When the world wearies, and society ceases to satisfy, there is always the garden.

—*Minnie Aumonier*

The Memory Jar

Throughout my childhood, my father and I always had a special bond, and we still do. As I look back, I have some wonderful childhood memories of some of the presents he gave me as tokens of his affection. Sometimes they were exotic gifts like a glowing jar of fireflies he captured while risking life and limb in a tall tree, or a pair of moccasins he swore were given to him by an ancient Indian chief (who, amazingly enough, wore just my size). Other gifts, however, such as the first gardenia blossom of the season from our flower garden, were simple and thoughtful and left just as lasting an impression on me. My family always had a beautiful flower garden, and of all the flowers we grew, gardenias were my father's absolute favorite. So, even at a young age, I knew the significance of being given one.

I loved all flowers, but I must really have cherished those gardenia blossoms because I would keep them well past their prime. I eventually started storing the dried blooms in a huge glass pickle jar I called my "memory jar." By keeping the dried petals, I think I was trying to store forever the memories of a little girl's special love for her father. If I was ever feeling blue or lonely, I would just open my memory jar and take a deep, fragrant breath. Somehow, that always seemed to cheer me up.

As I grew older and began attending dances and proms, I decided to dry all of the corsages and flowers I received from young boys and save them as well in my memory jar. Every special event throughout my teenage years that involved flowers was preserved in that jar of memories. I never knew exactly what I was going to do with this jar, but at the time it was nice to keep them as a token of the special moments and the special loves of my life. However, in time the memory jar was forgotten and tucked away somewhere in my closet.

Many years later, I met the man who was to be my future

husband. I immediately knew there was something special about him. For some unknown reason, the first time he gave me a bouquet of flowers, I thought of the memory jar. I decided to dry and save the flowers. Here I was, twenty-five years old, renewing a childhood tradition! But somehow, it just felt right. Thus I started a new memory jar in which I preserved every flower he gave me throughout our three-year courtship. When we did decide to marry, I was grateful that I had preserved so many mementos of our special moments.

We both enjoyed the outdoors, flowers, and gardening, so it seemed appropriate to have an outdoor wedding in my parents' abundant flower garden, the same garden I'd grown up with. I wanted to incorporate the garden theme throughout the entire wedding day. One of my ideas was to make a floral potpourri from all the flowers I had collected in my first memory jar and create fragrant sachets to be given to the guests at our wedding. It could be a symbolic way of saying good-bye to all the previous loves of my life.

My future husband loved the idea of giving away all the flowers I had received from other people, but what was I to do with all the flowers he had given me? Wanting to do something truly special with my fiancé's flowers, I decided to combine them with the gardenias that were at the bottom of my first memory jar and create a second potpourri influenced by the two most important men in my life. I combined this potpourri with some lace from my wedding gown and created two sachets. The first was sewn into the hem of my wedding gown so that I carried their love with me as I walked down the aisle. The second I placed in my hope chest to be passed on, as a family heirloom, to a future daughter or niece. And on our wedding day, the garden looked beautiful; even the gardenias were blooming.

I still have both sachets and they are a constant reminder of two of the most important bonds I have had in this lifetime: my father's love, which gave me confidence and guidance in my formative years, and my husband's love, which provides nurturing in my daily life and strength when times are tough. And when my husband and I tend our own flower garden, I always give special attention to the gardenias. Perhaps one day I will be able to present our son or daughter with the first bloom of the season as a token of my love for them.

Theresa Loe

Create a layered design with your favorite dried herbs and flowers. Use a glass jar or vase that is clear and smooth. Begin on the bottom and work your way up, creating flat, even layers of materials. Make your selections based on variety of color, shape, and size. These are wonderful choices: rosebuds, amaranth heads, eucalyptus leaves, everlastings, pressed zinnias, pressed black-eyed Susans, and pressed dogwood blossoms.

I have a garden of my own . . . shining with flowers of every hue.
I loved it dearly while alone, but I shall love it more with you.

— Thomas More

My Father's Roses

My father was my mentor and the man to whom I always turned in times of trouble, joy, or sadness. A man who had the right answer for everything, he seemed to be able to help all those he met.

His favorite pastime was his garden. Born in Germany, where gardens were not in fashion, in the thirties he emigrated to England, where tending the garden is practically a way of life. In no time, he fell in love with flowers, and they became an important part of his life. He enjoyed making sure my mother celebrated birthdays, anniversaries, and other special occasions with red carnations, one of his favorites.

My father had few hobbies, but as he progressed in life and moved from a smaller house to a bigger one, so grew his gardens and his passion for them. He cultivated whatever the land would allow and always won compliments for the way his gardens looked.

As he reached his mid-seventies and decided to retire, he moved again, this time to the United States to settle in Florida. What a most unlikely place for an English country garden! But he set about creating one for himself in his own clever way. The land and the climate, of course, did not allow for too much creativity, but he found that he could cultivate his favorite blooms, roses.

In practically no time, he had developed a beautiful rose garden in front of his house. Being a bit of a transplant himself, he was always delighted when passersby would praise it and exclaim, "There must be an Englishman living there. Who else could create such a rose garden in the heat of Florida!"

At age eighty-six, while working in his garden, he passed away. When I think of his passion for his flowers, I realize how fortunate he and many of us are to love something so engaging and so beautiful, and then spend our time nurturing and growing it for our personal enjoyment and the enjoyment of others.

Ron Wallace

On a sunny day the source of the overall smell of a garden can be found in the aroma of the volatile oils in leaves. The function of leaf scents is different from that of flowers. Flower fragrances are used to attract pollinators, while the leaf scents are used to discourage leaf-eating insects. While flower scents are beautiful and aromatic, leaf scents tend to be pungent, aromatic, medicinal, and intense. Try testing these smells on your next walk in the garden.

The breath of flowers is far sweeter in the air, where it comes and goes like the warbling of music, than in the hand.

—*Francis Bacon*

One Gentle Reminder

While my own talents seem to lie in speaking, performing, and writing, my admiration for people who create beauty with their hands is boundless. That's why I so admired everything my mother could do, from designing, painting, restoring, and constructing to planting and sowing. When I was three, we moved to a big, older house in the country, and its huge yard was nature's canvas for my artistic mother. Among the many, many creative things she did to the yard—never overdoing and always letting nature take its course—was a bed of lilies of the valley under a little arbor in the side yard. There was something dainty and secret about this beautiful small bed, just as there is something dainty and secret about those tiny, fragrant plants. To this day, I sniff hopefully through the offerings of perfume and cologne counters, ignoring heavy, manufactured scents in the hope of finding one gentle reminder of Mama's lilies of the valley.

Hope Mihalap

Vertical gardening can add drama to your garden. To create vertical interest, consider tree roses or climbers. Tree roses are rosebushes that are grafted onto special trunks of other types of trees of varying heights, from eighteen to forty-eight inches tall. Tree roses can be created with hybrid tea or floribunda roses, and even a few miniature versions.

For a formal look, group tree roses together to give a drive or a walkway direction or to frame an entry. When placed along a structure, such as a wall or a fence, tree roses will soften the hard edges and provide great color. In an informal landscape, tree roses are perfect for two-tiered planting, effectively "doubling" garden space.

Climbing roses also add vertical interest to a garden. Characterized by long, arching canes growing as high as fourteen feet, these roses add a breathtaking wall of color when attached to an arbor, fence, trellis, or front porch railing.

. . . the best celebrations . . . emphasize family traditions, but also borrow colorful customs from many lands, and eras to weave a rich tapestry of prayers, parties, giving and receiving, dining and decorating.

—Adelma Grenier Simmons

I Call Mom!

I'm one of those people who loves flowers, but as a speaker traveling around the country, I can't stay home or in a hotel room long enough to enjoy fresh ones, much less take care of them.

When someone mentions flowers to me, I visualize the silk kind, those inviting floral arrangements that make even the darkest rooms cheerful. But I do appreciate the beauty of fresh flowers and the enjoyment they bring. So, what do I do when I need them in my home for company or on my table for a party? I call my seventy-three-year-old mother. No, she doesn't *send* bouquets, she *creates* them.

All I need to say is, "Mother, I'm having a party Friday night for about sixty people, and I need something light and airy for the entryway table, something plum." And she's off—to a dozen stores to select the perfect combinations of roses, or lilies, or daffodils for the focal point, along with their necessary greenery, to be put in either the most delicate or elaborate vase. She's never had a course in floral arranging or read a book on the topic, yet she has the skill and taste to decorate any Ritz-Carlton in the world. As the years go by, and I have become involved with my own children, it becomes more and more important for my mother and me to find common bonds that provide the involvement we both need. For us, flowers are one of the answers.

Dianna Booher

Flowers are very delicate and should be handled carefully. Their petals and leaves may bruise, tear, or break off and stems can bend or break. Flowers are also sensitive to temperature changes. If too warm, food is used up too fast and water is lost more quickly than it can be replaced, which can lead to deterioration, wilting, and premature death.

More than half a century has passed, and yet each spring, when I wander into the primrose wood and see the pale yellow blooms, and smell their sweetest of scents . . . for a moment I am seven years old again and wandering in the fragrant wood.

—Gertrude Jekyll

Rites of Passage

The teenage years bring many rites of passage. In a way, one of those is the giving of a corsage. If the closest you have ever been to a flower is the patch of daylilies that forms the warning line in left field in the backyard Wiffle ball field, the thought process is mind-boggling. Why does this girl need one of these to go to a dance? Where do you go to get one? What do you ask for? How badly can your hands shake while trying to figure out how to pin it in the right place?

To become an adult and find yourself in a profession where a knowledge of flowers is taken for granted, the appreciation level alters 180 degrees. No longer is it a red flowery thing, but a cattleya, a member of the most spectacular family of flowering plants, the orchids. It is something that grows in the greenhouse in the backyard of the former ball player. Nor is it any longer a boutonniere, but a carnation, a flower whose history you can now recite flawlessly.

Along with adulthood can come parenthood, a process that begins with a tiny baby who is forever your baby. Parents may define the awakening of the loss of their baby in many ways, but certainly one is to see a fourteen-year-old in a formal dress for the first time, hair fussed over for hours, wearing eye shadow and lipstick. Next, a young man comes strolling up the walk holding a box in a way that lets you know he thinks something inside is ticking. But he presents it with grace and helps slip it onto her wrist—a corsage that will go into the refrigerator after this night and eventually be dried and added to the memories of youth.

Bill Aldrich

When ordering flowers for a busy holiday such as Christmas or Valentine's Day, don't wait till the last minute. The earlier you place the order, the more time the florist will have to create something unique. You may want to order the flowers in person and sign the card yourself as an extra-special touch.

The greatest gift of a garden is the restoration of the five senses.

—Hanna Rion

The Scent of a Woman

I woke up this morning to another beautiful fall day. The beautiful days of every season always remind me of the gardens tended by the women in my family.

I remember the African violets that grew in my grandmother's east-facing breakfast nook window. Every color of violet, single and double, she raised from tiny leaves to full plants. Since I've tried unsuccessfully as an adult to raise these flowers, I realize now that she had a real knack for growing them.

My mother's and grandmother's flower gardens had peonies that bloomed at Memorial Day and were taken to the cemetery. There were dahlias, fuchsias, ferns, lavender, rhododendrons, quince, black-eyed Susans, hollyhocks, and the ever-invasive morning glory. But the roses. Oh, their scent is still with me today!

There have been studies on how scents imprint the brain, and I believe that this is true for me. The tea roses are still growing in the gardens of my childhood even though the women who planted them are gone. When the fragrance hits my nose, the women appear in my mind, bringing with them fond memories of bonding experiences in my youth.

I recall how together we would prune the tender roses in the early spring, after the first frost. Then there was the magic of watching their first blossoming; how long a single raindrop could sit on a petal before it would run to a bloom's center; the careful cutting for bouquets—always near a five leaf. We enjoyed collecting nearly withered petals for making rosewater and rose beads. The last bloom, when the spiders wove their webs from plant to plant, was the beginning of the preparation of the rosebushes for the dormant season.

Those women gardeners grouped roses as climbers, floribundas, hybrid teas, and old garden roses. Some names I still recall, such as Dainty Bess, Peace, Tropicana, Crimson Glory, and Sutter. But there are the scents first, then the color combinations that remain with me today, bringing to mind the women whose influence shaped my life and filled my heart.

Patsy Moreland

The fragrance of flowers seems more romantic and mysterious at night. Since our visual sense is limited, the senses of smell and touch become more acute. Flowers with the most profound night scents include August lily, night-blooming jasmine, lady-of-the-night, and datura.

If you once loved a garden that love will stay with you.

—Louise Driscoll

Community Garden

I grew up in a small town where you could walk at night and not be concerned about your safety. The neighborhood children and I would routinely meet in my backyard every day for a game. From after school until sundown, my life consisted of hide-and-seek and freeze tag with kids I had known for as long as I could remember. While we children were occupied, the parents would socialize or take time for themselves. They would share their recipes, discuss the community's activities, and just unwind while the kids played together. I guess you could say that daily routines provided us with a sense of community that we found comforting.

One of my mother's routines was her daily walk. She would always walk the same path, on the same streets, in the same order. Each day she passed the house of a man who had very little in terms of material wealth, but whose front yard was what captured the eye. In addition to a multitude of amazing flowers, it was full of gorgeous irises, which were one of my mother's favorites. To talk to this man was to love his flowers. He talked about his passion for life and how he lived through his garden. "Every flower is unique," he explained. "Different colors, various life spans; it's almost as if they have their own personalities." Very much like people, I would think to myself.

In keeping with the sharing of our community family, one day when he was planting his bulbs for the season he stopped by our house and dropped off several for us to grow. Year after year the flowers continue to bloom. People from the neighborhood have moved away, new families have joined the town, the children continue their games of hide-and-seek, and the parents continue to socialize. Our friend passed away a few years ago, but his irises still grow.

Allison Lynn Ondrey

The iris is called a "form" flower. Its unique shape makes it a prime flower to use in the focal area of cut-flower arrangements. In the garden, beds of iris create striking demonstrations of color and shape.

Working in the garden gives me something beyond enjoyment of the senses . . . it gives me a profound feeling of inner peace. There is no rush toward accomplishment, no blowing of trumpets. Here is the great mystery of life and growth. Everything is changing, growing, aiming at something, but silently, unboastfully, taking its time.

—Ruth Stout

Snow Roses

My grandfather Harry was a grocer and an amateur horticulturalist, a man who really loved flowers. He even had his own greenhouse in his backyard. He grew roses and had several roses he had cultivated himself named after him. I grew up looking at those beautiful roses down in his greenhouse every time I visited him.

Harry had a large family, including several boys who at times teased their dad for spending so much of his time down in that greenhouse tending to his flowers. One day in the deep of winter, after a fresh snowfall, his sons—my father included—got an idea. The family home had a long front porch screened by an ivy-covered trellis that ran all the way around it. To anyone passing by the house after a new snowfall, the vine looked like a wall of snow surrounding the porch. The boys sneaked down to their dad's greenhouse and picked five dozen red roses, which they secretly arranged in the snow-covered ivy trellis. Then they went inside and started calling people on the phone, saying, "Did you see the beautiful red roses growing through the snow at Harry Vance's house?" My father told me there was a line of cars passing by the house for twelve hours, nonstop—full of people wanting to see Harry's unusual red roses that would grow through the snow!

Mike Vance and Lisa Wolf

Remains of roses have been found in Egyptian tombs. A red rose is pictured at the four-thousand-year-old palace at Knossos on Crete. The rose continues to be a symbol of love and purity.

There's rosemary, that's for remembrance;
pray you, love, remember.
And there is pansies, that's for thoughts. . . .
There's a daisy. I would give you some violets,
but they wither'd all . . .

—*William Shakespeare*

Forever Rose

My grandpa had died suddenly while vacationing with his children and their families. Many bouquets of flowers came expressing the loss of a good family man and friend. One particular bouquet of roses came from his life-long friend and coworker. After about a week, my mother noticed that one of the cut roses had begun to root—an unusual development for cut roses.

She decided to plant the rooted rose in front of their new home, recently built on the five-generation family farm that had been tenderly cared for by our late grandpa. The rosebush grew and grew, giving wonderfully fragrant roses to all of us. That was thirty-four years ago. As I cut and smelled the roses again this year, I told their story to my children to be passed along for one more generation—the living memory of a wonderful grandfather.

Lynnette Schuepbach

For flowers that bloom about our feet,
Father, we thank Thee.
For tender grass so fresh and sweet,
Father, we thank Thee.
For the song of bird and hum of bee,
For all things fair we hear or see,
Father in heaven, we thank Thee.

—*Ralph Waldo Emerson*

The Snowball Tree

My childhood home, the city of Chicago, was not exactly a place where you'd find meadowlands of blooming flowers, but I remember a particularly beautiful bush that grew outside our living room window. In the spring, the large bush would explode with tiny, white, fragrant flowers whose petals joined together in what looked like soft snowballs. We called it the snowball tree.

If you were Catholic, May was the month you honored Mary, the mother of Jesus. On the first day of May a ceremony called "May Crowning" was held, which consisted of one girl being selected to crown a statue of Mary with a ring of fresh flowers. All the girls were encouraged to bring bouquets of flowers to place on the altar for May Crowning, and throughout the rest of the month. Mother helped me carefully snip some blooms from the snowball tree, and when I brought them to their place of honor and respect, I truly felt like I had made a contribution.

It's interesting how some occurrences in our lives are completely forgotten, even if they happened just the day before, while others remain with us a lifetime. What causes this? Do colors, shapes, and scents make an unforgettable impact on our minds? It seems that way for me. I remember that amid all the colorful daffodils and lilacs, the pure white snowballs stood out in elegance and splendor. To this day, I've never seen another snowball tree, but I can still smell them in my memories when spring comes around.

Elizabeth Jeffries

Landscape and shrub roses are ideal for horizontal gardening, blending into any landscape and integrating with other flowers. A simple technique is to plant lower growers in front, with mid-high plants in the middle and tall varieties in the back. For harmony, choose similar colors and heights. Bold gardeners can break the rules and use taller varieties throughout a garden.

For a privacy screen that will keep nearby buildings and busy streets at bay, plant a hedge of shrub roses intermingled with grandifloral and floribundas. No fence could be more attractive. A grouping of landscape shrub roses will effectively hide eyesores like trash receptacles or wells.

There are myriad relationships continually going on unseen beneath the surface of the garden.

—*Bob Flowerdew*

THE FRIENDSHIP GARDEN

I first learned about "volunteer" plants from my grandma Nada, an avid gardener with a very green thumb. I was starting college and renting a house across the street from her, where I was planting a flower and herb garden. I remember the day she first asked me if I would like to have one of her "volunteer" impatiens for my garden. I was new to gardening and had no idea what a volunteer plant was, so I boldly asked, "What did the plant volunteer for?" After a good laugh, my grandmother explained that a "volunteer" was an extra plant that came up on its own. It was not planted intentionally, but was valuable because it could be dug up and given as a gift to a fellow gardener. Wow! What a wonderful way to expand a garden. I could gather volunteer plants and create a whole garden for free!

I enthusiastically took my grandmother's impatiens, and throughout the years accepted other volunteers such as foxgloves, violets, and geraniums from her thriving garden. I soon found I loved gardening, and before I knew it, my "hobby" had turned into a "profession," as I became a garden writer. I started teaching others about using the garden's bounty to beautify the home. As my horticultural knowledge and writing career grew, so did my circle of gardening friends; subsequently, my garden grew as well. I was given seeds, cuttings, and divisions, as well as "volunteers" from them. I soon accumulated a wonderful assortment of rare and unusual plants from around the world. And through my work as a garden writer, I was occasionally given new cultivars that were not readily available to the general public. Each plant became precious to me, and so, being a renter, I would either keep my plants in pots or I would dig up the entire garden and take it with me every time I moved.

When my husband and I bought our first home together, we had hundreds of potted plants and couldn't wait to start designing a more permanent garden. So, rather than work on fixing up the inside of our home, we opted to spend the first six months planning and planting the outside. We wanted to turn the entire backyard into a colorful cottage garden, complete with a meandering pathway and white picket fence, filled with all the herbs and flowers I had collected.

As I followed the garden plan and set each plant in its place, I began to reminisce about the person who had given me that plant. While I worked, I realized that my entire garden had actually evolved into a friendship garden. Almost every plant I had was attached to a fond memory and a special friendship. There was the double-delight rose given as a wedding gift by my sisters-in-law, the perennial morning glory from a dear friend in San Diego, the chocolate-scented cosmos from my sister, the silver sage plant from Texas, the hollyhocks from South Carolina, the sweet peas from England, and the oregano from Canada. Each plant had a special history and a story to tell about its giver.

I love my garden. Each day as I stroll through it, I brush my hands through a fragrant herb or stop to smell a delicate flower and feel as if I am visiting with all of my friends and family. I am struck by the memories and emotions tied to each plant. For this reason I am always careful to collect seeds, cuttings, and divisions so that others may share in the joy my garden brings to me. It also may provide a memento of a special time we spent together, and they will think of me each time they see that particular plant.

My grandmother is getting older, but she still gardens in a small area of her yard. We talk weekly about how the roses and fruit trees are doing and give each other the latest home remedy for insects. And not a visit goes by that we do not make some kind of plant exchange. I think that is the part of gardening that

I enjoy most—sharing with the woman who helped me build this garden of friendship in the first place.

Theresa Loe

If you wish to plant a biblical garden, here are some plants with biblical names: Jacob's ladder, Job's tears, Joseph's coat, false Solomon's seal, rose of Sharon, and Solomon's seal. You also might want to try planting these, which are found in the bible and are still available today: herbs—bay, coriander, garlic, hyssop, mint, mustard; fruits—apples, grapes, mulberries; trees—cedar, fir, oak, ash, sycamore; vegetables—beans, gourds, lentils, cucumbers, leeks, onions, radishes, and garlic.

Summer afternoon—summer afternoon;
to me those have always been the
two most beautiful words in
the English language.

—Edith Wharton

Twilight Evenings

Childhood memories of summer return as I search for the perfect spot to hang our hammock at our new house. During the hot days and nights of my childhood summers, my entertainment came in the forms of daisy chains, hickory whistles, and lightning bugs captured in Queen Anne's lace. I preferred these "toys" to fancy battery-operated ones.

Adults usually occupied the hammock on those twilight evenings, while I pursued the lightning bugs, which seemed to be at their peak at the same time that the Queen Anne's lace bloomed. I have always been fascinated by Queen Anne's lace, since each flower varies from the next. Some are flatter or whiter, while others have a dark purple spot in the middle, said to be a drop of blood from the queen's finger as she pricked it while working on her lace.

When dusk filled our backyard, I would try to capture the lightning bugs. If I were quick enough, I could trap one between two heads of Queen Anne's lace by holding the stems and bringing the wide, flat surface of the flowers together over the lightning bugs. I'd be able to possess my own little Tinkerbell that glowed just for me. Maybe our hammock will find a spot near my bed of Queen Anne's lace, where I can watch the girls from next door play with nature's own ever-ready light show.

Libbey Oliver

Red or White?

I grew up in a flower-loving family. My fondest memories of my late father are of him always giving my mother flowers—every holiday, and especially on their anniversary and Mother's Day. As a child, I remember Daddy making sure that my siblings and I always wore flowers to church on Easter, Mother's Day, and Father's Day. I hated it then, it was just one more part of "dressing up" that most young boys resented, but as an adult, I've never missed wearing one on those days. And since my dad is gone, we've made sure Mother still gets flowers at those special times.

We learned early on that a red rose on Mother's or Father's Day meant your mom or dad was still alive, and a white one meant they had died. I vividly remember riding to church with my parents who, in my childhood, wore red roses that gradually changed to white as the years progressed and each of my grandparents passed away. Each year, I was so glad I was wearing a red one. I also remember the first time I put on a white rose on Father's Day, and how every year for the past twenty-four years I've been able to honor my dad in that small way. I'm still wearing a red one on Mother's Day, but I know the day will come when it, too, will change to white. And every year when I put a small rose on my lapel on Mother's and Father's Day, I'll feel a little closer to the two people who brought me into this world, loved, and cared for me so much. Wouldn't it be nice if more people wore flowers for this reason?

Al Walker

Pressed Close to My Heart

My grandmother Marian was a wonderful letter writer whose letters would almost always arrive with a pressed flower tucked between their sheets of tissue-thin airmail paper. She had gotten in the habit of writing on the featherweight paper during the many years she spent in South America, where my grandfather was an agricultural adviser for the U.S. government. Her letters from Panama or Brazil would have nameless, but very exotic, tropical blooms whose once pure-white, fleshy petals would have turned golden brown and transparent by the time they reached me.

When my grandparents weren't out of the country, they spent their summers at their cabin in the mountains of Colorado. In the 1960s, mail service came only twice a week to the Crystal River Valley, so mornings before the mailman was due, we kids tried not to interrupt "Nen," as Marian was called by us grandchildren, as she wrote on the front porch. The creek babbling in the background and the aspen trees rustling overhead didn't seem to distract her. Her tea would get cold at her elbow as she concentrated on her correspondence, hurrying to finish "just one more letter."

The letters she wrote from the cabin usually had wild roses pressed in them. She would pick them on her daily walks from the bushes that grew abundantly along the dusty dirt roads. Some had very small, pale-pink petals, others huge, deep-pink ones, but all had the rich, musky fragrance that comes only from a wild rose.

Occasionally I would get a letter with silky buttercups or tiny forget-me-nots pressed between its pages and I would know even before I read it that she was visiting her brother at his ranch in Wyoming. There, her walks were down to the river, after the morning dishes were done. The pastures between the barns and the river were boggy places where she, the horses, the buttercups, and the bees were all happy. Knowing that there were always letters to write on her day's agenda, she would pick flowers on her way back to the house.

With the afternoon sun filtering onto her shoulders through the cottonwood trees and the enticing smell of pies in the oven, she would spend hours at the long kitchen table, writing. Most of the morning's collection of flowers would be pressed in a tea towel with a book on top, ready to add to the letter.

I can only guess at the reason she put flowers in her letters to me. Perhaps she wanted to share a precious part of her world with a granddaughter far away. Did she know I missed being with her on her walks? Was she thinking, "Here, my dear, is a rose just for you. I was thinking of you when I picked the prettiest one on the bush."

I can only assume that it was for the same reason that I went into my garden the morning I heard that my dearest Nen had passed away and cut armloads of flowers to fill every vase and jelly jar I owned and spent the rest of the day pressing flowers, and her, into memory.

My grandmother
Marian Myers Paschal
wrote this poem when her mother,
Nelle Myers, passed away.

Wildflowers

Mother, here are wildflowers,
I know you love them best.
Wild roses and rock lilies,
to grace your earthly rest.
I can't bring white carnations
in honor of your day,
You see, to me you are not gone
you're just a little ways away.
So, Mother, here are wildflowers
I've brought in a fruit jar vase,
Just as we always used to do
up at the old home place.

Ann Pettingell Wilton

UNEXPECTED SURPRISES

7.

The rose looks fair,

but fairer we it deem

For that sweet odour

which doth in it live.

—*William Shakespeare*

REAL MEN *DO* WEAR ROSES

Everybody knows that men don't like flowers; it's a given as strongly entrenched as their love for rough-and-tumble football. So why did they give me a white rose?

I suppose it was a nice gesture, but nice gestures should fit the person. As the meeting planner took to the platform to help lead the very kind standing ovation, she approached me with a single white rose and proceeded to pin it to my lapel; a thousand women applauded just a little bit louder. I gave a final wave to the audience and headed off the platform.

The keynote speech had gone well, but there was no time to enjoy the accolades. It was a long way to the airport, and I had a tight connection. Then again, such connections are par for the course for most speaking road warriors, and why should this day be any different? But that day it was different; there was that one little white rose that now shared my journey.

The pleasant smell of the rose filled the cab and all but masked the stale aroma of cigarettes long since put out. The cabbie asked a basic male question while looking into his rearview mirror: "You in a wedding or something?" After all, the only appropriate time for a man to wear a rose is at his high school prom or at a wedding. Since I look a bit beyond my prom years, a wedding was a good bet.

"No," I replied. "I think it was a reward for a good speech or a cover for a bad deodorant." His hollow laugh confirmed what I was privately feeling—that's not a good enough excuse for a man to wear a white rose! Real men don't wear roses unless they have to.

It was a relief to arrive at the new Denver airport and distance myself from the disapproving cabbie. I entered the long ticket line. Was I seeing things? I noticed women smiling at me as they glanced from my face to the flower and back to my face, lingering just a moment longer than usual. As a member of the over-the-hill gang, with a balding spot to prove it, looks like that were a welcome surprise. Had I lost weight? Unlikely. Are women in Denver desperate? It did not appear to me that these women could be desperate. No, but could it be the single white rose pinned to my jacket?

I was greeted by the ticket agent with a warm smile and an admiring comment: "What a beautiful white rose!" I thanked her for noticing as three other ticket agents joined the review panel to add their own supportive commentary on how good it was to see a man with a rose. Other men seemed to scowl, as if saying, "Who really cares!" Commenting on how pleasant my experience had been since putting it on, I left with a smile and a pleasant surprise: I had been upgraded, for free, to first class.

About the myth that men don't like flowers, I have one thing to say: My last count for research purposes indicates that all men minus one share that view!

Terry Paulson

The Prescription Is Flowers

Grandma was always surrounded by flowers. In her younger days, she and Grandpa had a large tract of land on the edge of town. Grandma had long rows of daffodils, peonies, gladiolas, zinnias, and dahlias as big as dinner plates. Large clumps of babies breath and asparagus fern made the field one beautiful bouquet.

Every week Grandma would bring large buckets of cut flowers home and fashion bouquets. Each one was tied with string and placed in water on the front porch, to be picked up by her customers.

All her life Grandma had flower gardens. Long after the "farm" had become a community of neat homes and professional florists' bouquets had replaced her home-grown ones, Grandma still grew lots of flowers, and her yard was a beauty to behold.

She still tended her flowers and mowed her lawn with her push mower when she was in her eighties, but cancer began to sap her strength, and she had to move to a nursing home. One day a friend called me and asked me to stop by on my way to visit Grandma. When I arrived, a large bucket of flowers was on the porch. Flowers of every color and shape had been tenderly grown and generously gathered by my friend's husband.

Gathering a basket of small jars, glasses, and vases, some scissors and a knife, I hurried to the nursing home. Grandma's face broke into the biggest smile I'd seen for a long time. Without a word, she set to work making that bucket of flowers into as many little bouquets as she could.

Proudly, she delivered the bouquets throughout the nursing home, bringing smiles to the other patients.

Each morning she got up, hurriedly dressed, and ate breakfast. She visited each room to freshen the water and discard the wilted flowers. Those flowers lasted for over a week, and later the nurse said Grandma didn't take any pain medication all the time she had those flowers to tend.

My friend could have sent Grandma a carefully arranged bouquet of lovely flowers, but the thoughtfulness and insight of sending her flowers she could arrange was an unparalleled act of kindness.

Eleanor A. Morgan

One of the most rewarding parts of gardening is gathering huge bouquets of flowers and bringing them indoors to enjoy. Flowers that do best for cutting are not always the same flowers that are best for landscaping. A cutting garden can be placed in a back corner of a landscape garden or even tucked along the edges of the vegetable garden.

When using a clear glass container for your cut flowers, fill it with stones, marbles, iridescent cellophane, or charcoal to provide a support for the stems or to conceal floral foam. Stained vases can be cleaned with a combination of vinegar and baking soda. Granulated toilet bowl cleaner is useful for cleaning lime-stained crystal vases.

Flowers are made to seduce the senses:
fragrance, form, color.

—*Hilda Doolittle*

The Garden Flower Corsage

I was a senior in high school and the fall homecoming dance was quickly approaching. There was no one special in my life at the time, and I figured I would just go with a female friend and have a blast. The only problem was that even to go with a friend, I still had to ask her. I kept putting off inviting someone to the big shindig until all of a sudden it was two weeks, then one week, before the dance. A bunch of guys in my situation had even started talking about not taking dates, just going stag and having a great time.

As the date drew nearer, my mother kept asking me if I was going, and if so, with whom. She was trying to plan ahead since she always made the corsages for my dates, and she wanted to be sure she had plenty of time to work her magic with the flowers. My answer to her varied from "Don't worry, I will find someone" to "I'm going with a bunch of guys, and we aren't taking dates." She continually reminded me to let her know in plenty of time so she could buy the flowers and accessories she needed.

She asked me every day the week of the dance, and when the day before the dance arrived without the announcement of a date, she assumed her services wouldn't be needed this time around. Finally, the night before the big event, I asked a girl who was in several of my classes and who would be fun to go with. She said yes, and I said to myself, "Hey, I knew I would get a date!" So that night I went home and told my mother. She freaked out! She had been at a conference all day and needed to be back at the conference by 8:00 A.M. the next morning. It was now 11:30 P.M. and all the possible places to purchase flowers and corsage makings were closed. "The night before the dance you find a date!" she said.

"Yes, but she doesn't need a corsage," I said.

"She'll be the only one there without one. How will she feel?"

"She won't care," I said. I really didn't think my date would care, but I also really didn't think it was possible for my mom to make one since she would be leaving early the next day and arriving home just around the time I would be leaving—no time to get flowers or make them into one of her creations.

But I drastically underestimated my mother. That night, my wonderful mom had an idea. She had already changed into her pajamas, slippers, and pink bathrobe. And this is how she was dressed when inspiration struck and she went outside and cut the last remaining roses off my father's rosebush in the front of the house. Since it was so late in the fall it was very unusual for there to be any roses left. With these last flowers of the season she managed to design the best corsage I had ever seen. More important, it seemed to be the most beautiful corsage *any* girl at the dance had ever seen. They just hovered around my date as she showed them her wrist. She was especially impressed that the flowers had been home-grown by my father and picked from our garden. They had a more beautiful fragrance than any that had come from a store. I was definitely wrong when I thought my date wouldn't care about not receiving a corsage, not when every other girl had one. She had managed to buy me a boutonniere that afternoon, and I would have felt like a real heel if my mom hadn't insisted on being sure that I followed the rules of corsage etiquette.

I really felt special that night, and I think it was because the flowers were grown with my father's care and arranged with my mother's love. I can't convey how much my date enjoyed the corsage, and when she heard how it came to be, she appreciated it even more. Big points for me! She and I wound up dating my entire senior year. I'd like to think it was because I was so irresistible, but, who knows, maybe it was the flowers.

Jim Lamancusa

I clearly remember the corsage-making night. I was really happy to have caught a glimpse of those pink roses on the rosebush, especially since I have a procrastinating child! It was so unusual for them to be in bloom that late in the season. Walking over, I smelled them and thought, "How lovely. What a gift of God." As the evening progressed I truly learned what a special gift of God they were!

You may want to be prepared in advance for your procrastinating child. Purchase a roll of green floral tape and a lace corsage wristlet from your local floral or craft shop.

A hot glue gun, a few silk rose leaves, and some thin corsage ribbon are also helpful. Just keep these on hand, they don't spoil. When you need to make the corsage, simply cut the roses from the rosebush so they have one- to two-inch stems. I like to use six roses per corsage with some of them being more open than others. Wrap the stems with the green floral tape to seal them, then glue the stems to the top of the lace corsage wristlet. Glue silk leaves and fresh leaves around the rose heads. Add a ribbon bow in the center of the corsage. If you can't tie a florist's bow, just tie a few bows the same way you tie your shoe and glue them together in the center.

Certainly, the preferred thing to do is to order the corsage from the local florist in plenty of time, but when in a pinch, hit the garden. Perhaps you, too, will end up being a hero to your child like I was!

Every flower is a soul blossoming out to nature.

—*Gerard de Nerval*

Canadian Spring

I live in Canada, the frozen north, where the first blooms of spring are much anticipated. Recently, we suffered through six full months of winter. The frost had penetrated so deeply into the ground that water mains had frozen solid and pipes were bursting in peoples' homes. On one occasion, we awoke to snow so high that the only indication in the drive of the burial place of our car was a slight hummock in the blanket of white. The cat didn't even bother to stand wistfully at the door anymore! Even for the hardiest of Canadians, it was depressing.

And then, finally, in April there was just enough of a thaw that we could see the snowdrops blooming under the cover of snow. Delicate white pendants with their lacy green edging, so tenacious in the icy soil. Soon, the purple and yellow crocuses and the pale blue scilla followed; and at long last, spring broke through. Watching the flowers gave us the daily reminder we needed that this winter would soon come to an end and that we would again experience the awakening of spring. Sometimes when we are feeling the most overwhelmed it takes something seemingly insignificant to provide the tiny spark of hope we need.

Susan E. Warkentin

Dandelion Magic

I once dated a college student who was so broke that we could afford to do very little in the way of entertainment. Mostly, we spent time together, much of it at a nearby park. We picnicked, walked, and talked about everything, including wishes that we made by blowing the fluff off dandelions. My mother always told me that my wishes would come true if I could blow off all their fluff with just one breath.

One day as I sat at my desk at work, he brought me a gift of potential wishes. A trip to the florist had provided him with floral fixative and foil. Flower pot, shovel, and florist supplies in hand, he visited our park. He "fixed" and potted some of our dandelions, fancied them up with the foil, and attached a card that read "May all your dreams come true."

His resources were limited, but the effects were magical. I often remind myself that the supplies for our dreams are at hand and only take a new perspective—and a little firing up—to be realized.

Nancy Grizzle as told to Michael Webb

Long, before there was a Valentine's Day, people linked the beauty and fragrance of flowers with ideas of love and romance. The Greeks and Romans had a love story for almost every kind of flower.

The Four-Thousand-Mile Hug

As I was being wheeled into my room after surgery that repaired a badly broken leg, the reality of what had happened started to sink in. My sons and I had survived a head-on crash with a tractor-trailer rig. The older one, Joe, was still in critical, but stable, condition after surgery, with severe internal trauma and a yet to be diagnosed broken back. My younger son, Jim, suffered from internal bleeding that was stopped through surgery as well. Our driver was recovering in a ward down the hall. My wife, Kathy, not having been in the accident, was probably the most hurt of all. She had to hear of the tragedy and the fact that she had almost lost her entire family. The realization that there would be months of recuperation after the initial emergency care we were receiving had already forced her into a care-giving, protective role. All this plus the fact that we were four thousand miles from home had my mind spinning! We were on a combination business/family vacation trip to England when our lives were changed.

The word spread back home that there had been an accident. Friends and family, business associates and clients wanted to touch us, comfort us, and help us. The distance was definitely a problem, as was the fact that the three victims were all in various stages of recovery and that Kathy was expending all of her energy caring for us and working with the various caregivers in an unfamiliar medical system.

The next day, it started.

An orderly wheeled into my room a cart carrying a beautiful floral arrangement. The card in it said simply, "We're thinking of you. Come home soon." It was from my brother and sister-in-law. I had it placed on a counter. It was then that I realized what a dreary place my room was. In the only semiprivate room on the floor, Jim and I were surrounded by off-white cinder-block walls in a hospital that had been built in the late 1800s. What a beautiful addition that single arrangement was.

That afternoon, two more arrangements arrived, one from my parents, one from Kathy's. We sent one to Joe's room and kept one in ours. The next morning, three arrangements were rolled into my room, these from friends and a professional-growth organization that Kathy belonged to. The messages were all similar: "We can't be there with you, but we're thinking of you," "This is the best way I can think of to send a four-thousand-mile hug," "May God take care of you and bring you home safely."

More flowers came that afternoon, and for the next week. Our rooms had so many flowers that we started giving some to the nurses who were caring for us. They were touched by our generosity.

Once I was feeling a bit better, some of our English friends and business associates started to visit. They were overwhelmed by the sheer amount of color and life, and the messages of love the flowers expressed. About a week after the accident, a man and a woman came through our door. I didn't recognize them. They introduced themselves as the florists down the street who had been the beneficiaries of the many wire-service orders of flowers that were to be delivered to us. In their own mild, gentle way, they said that they wanted to meet the family from America with so many friends and so much family. They were sure that we were "famous." I assured them that we were not, but that we certainly felt fortunate to be loved and missed. I also told them that we were lucky to have such a talented florist who could listen to the expressions of grief and sorrow from so far away and turn those feelings into beautiful floral messengers.

Our physical injuries have long since healed, but I will never forget the feeling I had when that cartful of flowers would arrive each day with messages and hugs from home.

Joe Lamancusa

Beauty alone is useless unless it reflects
the experiences of living.

—*Virginia Castleton Thomas*

Flowers for a Flute Player

They were roses, a lovely salmon color, and my girlfriend, Pam, loved them. So, naturally, I gave her some for her enjoyment. But flowers are not meant to be hidden or kept to oneself, they are best shared, so Pam not only placed them around her apartment but also took some to her workplace.

A homeless woman often lingered around the building where Pam works. She would sit in front of the building playing her flute. Her tunes were pleasant, but the woman kept to herself, rarely talking, content to play her flute in the sun. Once in a while, she would enter the building and use the lavatory for washing up. On this particular day, she walked past Pam's office where the salmon roses sat in a vase. She looked longingly at them. Noticing her, Pam got up, took some of the roses out of the vase and presented them to her. The woman had difficulty believing they were for her. Her eyes widened as she smiled the happiest of smiles. Pam said she literally "glowed."

The flowers brightened her day, and touched her in a special way that words never would.

Steve Rittner

All my hurts my garden spade can heal.

—Ralph Waldo Emerson

"Demon" Roses

My parents live on property inherited from my paternal great-grandmother, a feisty little lady very much tied to the land. She had been in failing health for several years and was living in a convalescent center when my parents moved into her house. Planted by her in the early days of her marriage, the property included fruit orchards, vegetable plots, and flower cutting gardens. Each had its place and purpose, except for her "demon" roses. This old-fashioned running rosebush was planted along the edge of the driveway, often obstructing the view of cars approaching the house.

When my mother moved in, she became determined to rid the yard of this plant. One year she pruned it back to a rather handsome bush, only for it to become vastly overgrown again during vacation time. Another year, she chopped it back to the ground, only to have it return more vigorous than ever. She even convinced my father to tie the root mass to the tractor and pull it from the ground, but back it came. As children, my siblings and I would often pick its pale-pink, single blooms for presents to our mother. She happily accepted our gifts in spite of the ongoing war that ensued every spring.

When I was away at college, she finally won the war. Radical pruning, spraying, and even rocks piled on the area finally rid the drive of the rosebush. The grass around the area was reseeded and developed into the plush lawn area my mother had always envisioned.

Several years later, my great-grandmother passed away. The next spring we noticed little sprouts in the yard: Her roses were back. It seems that during the time they were being mowed each summer, they were regaining strength and putting out new root structures, only to erupt again aboveground at her death. My mother, now older and wiser, gladly accepted their return and has at last made peace with the "demon" roses, an angelic reminder of my great-grandmother.

Michael A. Raburn

Flowers can surprise and delight those we love. They can send messages to family, friends, and associates. Flowers are like little angels from heaven that can supply a long-distance hug when we most need to send one. To send a message of romance, at night place a flower tied with a bow on the pillow of the one you love. To add the beauty of fragrance to the life of a friend, arrange a few stems of fragrant flowers just above the visor in their car. Even after the flowers have wilted, the aroma will last for several days.

Baby's Violets

My mother invited me to join her on a return visit to her native Texas. She had not been back in quite a while, and her oldest brother, Durwood, was seriously ill. His life had not been an easy one. He had enlisted in World War I when he was very young and had been gassed. Although it didn't prevent him from working as a rancher and raising a family, he suffered from respiratory problems for the rest of his life.

As we approached the nursing home, my mother picked some wild violets and formed a tiny bouquet. Now eighty-two, Durwood was lying in bed with failing eyesight, unable to see much beyond light and shadow. He visibly brightened when he heard my mother's voice. "Baby," he said with warmth. That was his nickname for my mother, his youngest sister.

Mom then placed the bouquet of violets under his nose and wrapped his fingers around their stems. His eyes may have been failing him, but he instantly noticed the flowers' fragrance. Silently, he inhaled the aroma of the blooms slowly and deeply; and as he did, his face was transformed by calmness and delight. It was as if the bouquet was a key that unlocked hundreds of memories. My grandmother had always had violets growing in her yard, and the children would frequently scoop up a bunch of them with which to surprise her. Durwood closed his eyes, as if to hold fast the memory. He crushed the violets to his nose and breathed deeply again, savoring the fragrance. "Oh, Baby," he said with his eyes closed, "it *is* a beautiful world."

Dona Abbott

My friend Kath Bretherick, a renowned florist in England, shared a funny story about when and how she learned that violets "drink through their faces." She had to make a wreath covered with violets for a funeral. It was five feet across and so big that she had to balance it on four chairs. Kath remembers sitting on the floor inside the design to do the foliage edging. The local furniture delivery service had been contracted to deliver the design to the funeral home since they had the only truck large enough. Because of its size and the number of hours it would take to make, the wreath had to be made the day before the funeral. When Kath returned the next morning, she was shocked to find that many of the violets had collapsed and were drooping! Not quite sure what to do, she relied on the old stand-by trick of revitalizing flowers with a heavy misting of water. Before long, fortunately, they recovered. Through this experience, she learned that some flowers drink through their faces and need to have water on their petals as well as their stems.

There is a misconception that all flowers and plants—although beautiful—also have a lovely aroma. The reality is that some plants and flowers, do, others don't, and the aroma of still others can even be on the offensive side. If you are looking to add more fragrance to your yard, think about adding some of these plants. Not every variety of every flower listed will have a lovely fragrance, but you can start your planning with this list: alyssum, artemisia, butterfly bush, candytuft, chamomile, crocus, daffodil, daylily, flowering tobacco, freesia, gardenia, geranium, honeysuckle, hyacinth, iris, jasmine, lavender, lemon balm, lemon verbena, lilac, mint, narcissus, petunia, primrose, sage, sweet pea, and violet.

He who plants a garden plants happiness.

—*Chinese proverb*

Roses on Wheels

As a mother of seven children, six of them boys, celebrating Mother's Day is quite an event. My husband orchestrates the day, which begins with breakfast in bed. Then before it is time for church, the children are let loose outside to collect flowers from the field and my garden. In previous years I would tell the children to not pick some of my more prized flowers, but that only alerted them to the more exotic blooms.

Their offerings are then put into seven different vases. From these vases I choose seven flowers to create a corsage to wear during the day. Yes, dandelions, violets, and peonies can be combined into exquisite wearable art.

This past Mother's Day was one that I will never forget. While the younger ones were collecting fistfuls of blossoms from the front yard, my seventeen-year-old went to the back where his wildly painted van was parked. He opened the door and proceeded to spend a few moments collecting something. As he approached me, I saw that he held a bouquet of the most vivid roses I had ever seen. He was employed in the garden section of a local discount store, and I thought it was so nice of him to present me with some roses. But it wasn't only that. He led me to the back of his van, and with a flourish revealed that it was bursting with rosebushes!

I was speechless! It took a few days to plant the bushes. In fact, we had to give some of them to our neighbors. As for my Mother's Day corsage, it will remain a tradition, but after last year we are thinking of imposing some limits—my suggestion is that choices only come from stock "on hand"!

Leslie Hartsock

THE SECOND-CHANCE ROSE

Six months had passed since the devastating breakup with my beau of several years. He wasn't just "any" boyfriend—he was my high school sweetheart, my first real kiss, my first real date, and my escort to the senior prom. And, I thought, the only man I could ever love. Our relationship survived attending colleges in different states but didn't survive graduation, when, after much soul-searching, we decided to go our separate ways.

I prayed long and hard and asked God to please send me someone else—someone *He* would choose for me, someone who would love me intensely and enough to do foolish things for me. And, I wanted to be given a rose as a sign. I'd received flowers from friends, family, and old boyfriends on special occasions, but never roses "just because."

My friends urged me to stop feeling sorry for myself, so I decided to use the money I'd been saving and take a tour of Europe. Jokingly, I announced, "I'm going over there to get a husband." In reality, I wasn't ready for that at all. The emotional wound was still open, exposed, and raw. All I wanted was to forget about the prospect of marriage and just have some fun. I'd accepted the idea that I'd probably remain single for a very long time—if not my entire life—so I might as well enjoy it.

During my travels I met Bill, a quiet engineer from Fort Wayne, Indiana. Whenever our tour guide would pair off groups for scheduled activities, we'd be together. In less than a week, he'd gained my friendship and my trust—and my wallet and my passport.

When we got to Rome, the tour guide warned us that pickpockets were prevalent in Rome, and that ladies were at risk. He even said that thieves would go so far as to reach inside a woman's brassiere to grab a wallet, and more. A gentleman's front pants pocket was a different matter. "The thieves," he said, "don't go *that* far." So we ladies were advised to pair with a gent and have him put our valuables in his pocket. Bill willingly obliged, and kept my wallet and passport for safe keeping.

During our guided tour of the Coliseum, Bill and I became separated. Bill joined a group daring enough to climb to the top to take pictures. I stayed halfway down, out of the blistering Italian sun.

Half an hour or more had passed and the tour guide was shouting, "Last call! Everybody back on the bus!" Bill was nowhere to be found. Most of our group was headed down the steps of the Coliseum and back on to the bus. Still no Bill! I became frantic. My palms were sweating. "What on earth have I done? How could I be so foolish?" I had given all my money and my identification to a man I barely knew, and the bus was headed for France. I was praying again. "Dear God! Please bring him back with my money and my ID!"

As the bus pulled out of the parking lot, a fellow in the back shouted, "Look! There's a guy running alongside the bus!" The driver didn't stop. Several people jumped up and yelled, "Stop! Stop! He's trying to catch the bus!" Red-faced and nearly out of breath, Bill jumped up the steps and on to the bus and headed my way. I heard laughing and cheering, but I didn't want to look at him. I was mad and upset. How could he be so irresponsible as to run off with my things and keep an entire busload of people waiting? I just didn't think there'd be any excuse good enough.

That was until I saw what he was carrying. "Here," he said, "this is for you. I just had to get it for you." He handed me a single long-stemmed orange rose. I was speechless. "I saw the flower vendor's cart when I was up at the top of the Coliseum," he explained, "and I had to go the back way around to get on that side street so I could surprise you. I thought I had enough time. I could see the bus pulling away, and I ran all the way back here. I hope you're not angry."

How could I be angry? What he had done was awfully sweet and awfully foolish!

Our friendship and love grew, despite the fact that we lived in different states. It wasn't until nearly two years later, when we were planning our wedding, that I told Bill just how special that rose really was. Now, fifteen years and two kids later, we're even happier than we were back then. I know without a doubt, and with a rose, that Bill is indeed the man God handpicked for me.

Terri Quillen

Clear, round, glass containers, often called bubble bowls, of various sizes grouped together, can be used as a centerpiece. Fill the bowls with preservative-filled water and float the heads of flowers along with floating candles. Use only hearty flowers such as orchids, lilies, roses, and mums. Flowers with thin, delicate petals, such as daisies or freesia, may become water-soaked and damaged.

Live in each season as it passes; breathe the air,
drink the drink, taste the fruit, and
resign yourself to the influences of each.

—Henry David Thoreau

A Locker Full of Roses

I grew up in a very small town, and my mom was a beautician in a local beauty shop, so, for the most part, these two factors kept us basically in line and out of trouble. My parents were pretty strict with my sister and me. I, being the elder, probably felt more of their strictness than she did. Needless to say, I was discouraged from having a boyfriend until I was able to date, at sixteen. However, being discouraged and the reality of the teenage years are two different things. I was fourteen, almost fifteen (this distinction being important to a young girl), and the boy who asked me out was seventeen. I was open with my parents about his date inquiry. I assured them that I told him I couldn't date until I was sixteen. This information put my parents at ease—at least for a while.

The boy, on the other hand, obviously wasn't going to let the "no-dating" rule get in his way. Our crush turned into puppy love, and on Valentine's Day my freshman year, I opened my locker to find a bouquet of a dozen yellow roses. He was serious! I was terrified! What did this young man expect of me now? Did this mean we were "going steady"? I was afraid to go home with the flowers, but I swallowed my fear of the unknown and took them home anyway.

I walked across the street to the beauty shop, where Mom was working that day, and did the "Guess what happened today?" routine. To my dismay, the word had already spread, reaching my mom before I could. And besides, I was beaming! How many blossoming teenage girls get a dozen yellow roses from their first boyfriend? From then until the end of our short-lived relationship, my parents watched me like hawks.

Throughout the remainder of my teenage years and into college, that young man had set a standard by which all my other boyfriends were measured.

Finally, in college, I met the man who would become my husband. Dennis made me realize the more important standards in life: God, family, and self-confidence. He has given me many kinds of flowers over the course of our relationship, representing our constantly changing life. We are now expecting our first child. All the experiences that go with becoming parents are causing us to grow closer than I ever thought would be possible.

Amy Doggett-Burns

A LIFE IN FLOWERS

8.

THE EARTH CAN BE AN ABUNDANT MOTHER IF WE LEARN TO USE HER SKILL AND WISDOM—TO TEND TO HER WOUNDS, REPLENISH HER VITALITY, AND UTILIZE HER POTENTIALITIES.

—*John F. Kennedy*

Keep the Change

I was busily preparing my shop for another day, mindful that we would present quality flowers and plants, carefully wrapped, at an affordable price, and still make a profit. I looked up as the door chimes announced the arrival of a customer. Well, actually three customers. Big brother, Michael, was about eight years old. As usual, the girl was "in charge"—Susan was about six. And four-year-old baby brother, Tommy, was there because he always had to tag along—and besides, he had the money.

It seems it was Mom's birthday and they wanted to buy a plant. It had to be beautiful. It had to be "this big"—very big with a very, very big bow. Could I wrap it up in a big bag so they could hide it until supper?

A couple of inquiries determined that they had seven dollars and eighty-seven cents. Actually, Tommy had the $7.87, and it was safely in his pocket.

We set to work to find the perfect plant—this one too big, that one not big enough. Finally, the plant with the pretty pink flowers seemed perfect. Now for the bow! Michael wanted red. Susan insisted that would look "yucky," that yellow would be better. So we compromised and made it yellow *and* red. All this time, Tommy was quiet—but he had the money.

Would I put our big gold label on the bag? Of course. Michael chose the card. The one with the puppy dog on it because Mom loved puppies, didn't she? All signed their names. They had to hurry. Mom would soon be finished at the grocery store next door.

We quickly placed the plant in a big brown bag—in case she came in before they were ready. Now, all that was left was to pay. Here is where Tommy was needed. "How much?" they asked.

"It comes to $7.75," I answered, thinking to myself, "No profit on that sale!" Tommy carefully pulled out the money from his pocket—crumpled bills, lots of sticky coins—and together we counted out $7.75. He was left with twelve cents and a big dilemma.

Michael and Susan had had the idea to buy the plant, but it was all his money. What should he do with the change? Michael and Susan were already on their way to the door with the big, bulky package as he began to put the change back in his pocket, still a bit troubled. I looked over at Tommy, barely as tall as the counter.

"Is everything okay?"

"Oh yes, it's pretty, but . . ."

I waited. The little voice finally said, "Lady, do I have to give you a tip? No?"

What a relief! The coins were quickly stashed deep in his pocket and off he ran to catch up with Michael and Susan—secure in the knowledge that he hadn't had to spend everything!

Indeed, florists do turn feelings into flowers, and you even get to keep the change. What a lucky mom! What a lucky florist!

Sylvia P. Nichols

Want to send flowers to someone special, but not sure what kind to send? Most florists are members of nationwide wire service organizations that provide selection guides to make your shopping easier, and to ensure that you know what will be sent. Simply visit the local florist and peruse the selection guide when ordering. Whether the design you select is to be delivered in your own city or across the country, you'll have the reassurance that what you send will look very similar to what you chose from the selection guide. So you don't forget those special times that warrant flowers, why not place a standing order for the year? Then, the flowers will arrive on time and you won't have to remind yourself to send them!

Flowers are words which even
a babe may understand.

—*Bishop Coxe*

Flower Children

You often hear florists referring to their children as being "raised under the design bench." The phrase evokes a Norman Rockwell–like image of a small family-owned shop with children sleeping in a cut-flower box while Mom and Dad work until dawn making funeral arrangements. The only latchkey was the key to the shop's back door where the kids could pop in after school and find their parents hard at work in the heady fragrance of the flowers standing in a "pool" of crisp, green stems. "Sweep up," Dad would say. And they did.

My daughter, Hilary, was a child born into this world. When she was about two, she quietly watched her dad hang Christmas lights and garlands on every unadorned inch of the flower shop in preparation for his holiday open house. Shortly after, we took her to the city to see the blocks of buildings festooned in lighted decorations. Wide-eyed, she pointed a small finger at the dazzling buildings and asked with childlike innocence, "Daddy do?"

When she was older, she handed out roses at that same holiday open house, wearing a velvety dress and smiling shyly. She was the runner for the driver at holidays (a biker guy by night, with a beat-up Harley, a scraggly beard, and a big heart). She vacationed at floral conventions and made box lunches for the crew on busy Saturdays. When her class studied basic botany, she hauled in enough old flowers so that everyone could dissect the stamens and pistils until they got it right.

When you're busy raising your children, you don't think much about how these little everyday experiences will affect them later in life. But they do. They learn about the rewards of hard work, the beauty of nature, the uselessness of waste, and the diversity of people. The lessons learned are important.

When the time came, Hilary, never interested in floristry as a career, moved to the mountains of Colorado to study commercial art. But suddenly, last spring, she announced that she wanted to work in a flower shop. After recovering from the shock, my only advice was to get a job in a really great shop. Within a week, she had signed on at a magnificent studio shop in Aspen, Colorado, a community that caters to celebrities and tycoons and brags of the best skiing and the priciest real estate in the United States.

I visited her for the first time a few weeks ago; she was making an arrangement for the cliff-clinging home of a prince of a major oil-producing country—a shop regular. The pace at this shop is incredibly fast, the clientele is star-studded, and the owner can orchestrate a six-figure floral event flawlessly with her crew of artsy, Generation X designers.

In my wildest dreams, I never imagined my daughter making flower arrangements for a prince, but she has never been happier (or busier). Whether your children end up in the floral business, or following in your professional footsteps, whatever your career may be is irrelevant. But what is important is that by "raising them under the design bench," you have instilled in them the crucial values needed to lead an honorable and productive life.

Frances Dudley

Keep a bouquet of fresh flowers lasting longer by using a clean vase for them. Remove all the leaves that will be underwater. These submerged leaves will decay, creating bacteria and shortening the life of the flowers. Recut the stem of each flower underwater before placing it in the vase. This prevents air pockets from forming that block the water uptake to the flowers. Recut the stems every three days. Add floral preservative, also known as fresh flower food, to the water in the vase. Top off the vase water daily and change it every few days. Always place your bouquet in a draft-free location away from harsh sunlight or heating vents.

Calla Lilies

As a professional florist as well as a vocational and academic instructor at a local public high school in Westminster, Colorado, I often provide custom flowers for a wedding or a special event for students or staff members in the community. As I browse through the design books, magazines, and assorted literature/portfolios, I always come across designs with calla lilies. It is a flower that always brings me back to my early childhood growing up in Salinas, California.

As a child, my mother, Kyoko, would pile the neighborhood kids into our old white station wagon and drive to the local cemeteries, both Japanese and American. Once there, she would teach us how to place flowers on all the deceased servicemen's graves for each holiday, especially the traditional ones honoring those who served in the past World Wars, Korea, and Viet Nam. My American father was a captain in the United States Army who retired at Fort Ord and belonged to all the local chapters of the VFW, the American Legion, and the DAV.

On these trips, the flower she used most often was the calla lily. She had them growing in our entire yard, both back and front. She was always splitting them and placing them in a spot that had been left unused. Since she never used pesticides, she would pinch all the snails off the plants by hand and throw them in the garbage can. Whenever I took the trash out, I was careful when lifting the lid off the old metal cans because of the snails nestled on the underside of the lids. My sister and I would scream at the sight of the snails when we opened the garbage cans, having forgotten what was on the inside. Whenever we placed the cut flowers in the car for delivery to the cemeteries, no one would sit far in the back, thinking the snails would attack. For years, we would be grossed out by the sight of a garden snail. I even began to dislike the calla lily because of the snails. As we got older, we laughed at the thought of how we had been exposed to a ritual like this, and how harmless snails are to humans.

It was my college instructor Bob Gordon who finally showed me the beauty of the calla lily. In class, he had students cut their own flowers for their critiqued and graded designs from the numerous fields surrounding the campus. The calla lilies were always available, and they were beginning to make a comeback in the design world. He showed us the unique designs that could be created with calla lilies, which added a sense of drama. Today, callas are one of the most popular flowers because of their simplicity and beauty. They provide great lines for high-styled designs, or are bountiful and unique in a vase by themselves. I'm hooked and now appreciate their simple beauty.

As I flash back to my childhood, I am reminded of how simple life was back then. I am also reminded that while my Japanese mother was very patriotic and strove to be a good American citizen, she was also a survivor of the atomic bomb dropped on Nagasaki, Japan, which ended World War II.

Many of our dear friends at the Lincoln Avenue Presbyterian Church in Salinas, with a strong Japanese-American congregation, were interned during this war, even as third- or fourth-generation Americans. And yet, after surviving those years of internment, many returned to the Salinas Valley and became successful international flower growers and shippers. I am fortunate to have been exposed to the world of flowers, and realize that I have stories and memories of an era that was both special and unique.

Daily, as I teach my high school students, I tell them stories about flowers and the people who use them. I tell them about the bride who had the most beautiful bouquet or the funeral that celebrated the life of a loved one. I have them share their stories as well, and help them to realize that if they don't have a story, they soon will. At the end of a school year, the students have memories of a time that we shared that will be with them forever.

Flowers represent many things, and with them come armfuls of memories to cherish and be retold to future generations. Hopefully, our generations to come will not forget what took place so many years ago, and that flowers can play an important part in our daily lives, celebrating both life and death.

Jacquelin H. Dannemiller

When cut, daffodils have a sappy secretion that flows from the cut end. This secretion is harmful to other flowers, especially tulips, when exhibited in the same vase as the daffodils. To eliminate this, allow the daffodils to be in a vase by themselves for at least six hours or overnight. Daffodils can then be mixed with other flowers in fresh preservative-filled water without harm. Do not recut the daffodil stems before adding other flowers or the sap will begin to run again.

Boiled Roses

A husband came to buy twelve red roses for his wife. It was most important to him that the roses be fresh and of a superior quality, as his wife loved flowers but he had always found it difficult to please her.

A dozen nice, red roses were selected and carefully wrapped.

The next morning, a very distressed and angry wife called to complain that half of the roses had drooped and their heads were hanging.

We explained how to wrap the roses in newspaper and first hold them in boiling water for thirty seconds and then immediately place them in cold water (a much-used method twenty-five years ago). She was happy to try this procedure, and all problems seemed resolved.

The next morning, the lady turned up in the shop with a newspaper-wrapped bouquet of roses that were quite dead. She explained that she had boiled the roses as she was told and could not understand her results—black, very dead roses.

With great difficulty we kept straight faces and gave her twelve new red roses, having realized that she had boiled the heads instead of the stems!

Poul Einshøj

According to an old English legend, a rose can help a young girl find a husband. In Victorian times, husbands used small rose bouquets called "tussie-mussies" to communicate devotion, trust, and love. An anniversary tussie-mussie today could contain the number of red roses representing the months or years a couple has spent sharing happy moments together.

If you take any flower you please and look it carefully over and turn it about, and smell it and feel it and try to find out all its little secrets . . . you will discover many wonderful things.

—*Gertrude Jekyll*

Ralph's Final Lesson

I married into the Cleaver family; no that's not my last name, but an explanation of my in-laws. My mother- and father-in-law were the quintessential representation of the family of the 1950s. I often said that if anything happened and my marriage of twenty years did not work out, I wanted custody of my husband's parents. How can I explain, in today's world, these lovely people? Marie bakes from scratch, her home is always spotless, and she can craft anything. Ralph never acquired a high school education, but was more intelligent than over half the college graduates I know. He could make anything and do anything. He was loving, giving, and always quick to help others. I have been blessed because these two wonderful people, who, by the way, have a pretty terrific son, enthusiastically supported our endeavors. They have helped raise our two children. Marie has baked cookies for school and made Halloween costumes. Ralph built dollhouses and supervised science projects.

I have lived that white-picket-fence life and have adored the traditions that go with it. But this year, everything changed in an instant. I remember that my husband, Mark, our two daughters, and I were at home around the dinner table when the phone rang. Mark's face had the strangest look on it. He spoke in less than audible tones: "That was the ambulance. Dad has collapsed. They are taking him to the emergency room. They won't let Mom ride with them." I'm sure Mark said something after that, but I just can't recall what it was. Ralph was gone in an instant. . . . You are shocked, you are angry, and yes, it isn't fair.

Marie, Mark, Kim, Mark's sister, and I went to the funeral home to make the arrangements. We planned a simple family viewing and graveside service on a Monday morning. The people at the funeral home were kind. The newspaper did a feature obituary that was a quarter page. Of course, I would do the flowers.

I've owned a flower shop for sixteen years and floral design is my passion. But I have to honestly admit that when it comes to funeral flowers, I have had difficulty. I always had, in the back of my mind, the spending of all that money for such a short period of time. Was it really worth it? The flowers for Ralph's funeral were few, just a casket spray, two intertwined hearts, an easel, and a fireside basket. The arrangements were constructed from whatever was already in my cooler. I was too upset and, to be honest, after many years of enjoying flower buying, I was just not in the mood. I cried the whole time I made the arrangements. Mark bravely offered to come to the store with me, but he couldn't remain in the room while I worked. It was therapeutic for me to be able to do these flowers for Ralph. He had always enjoyed and encouraged my work.

Anxious to have the service behind us, the family arrived at the funeral home before the flowers. We sat in the cold chapel with Ralph, in an uncharacteristically quiet pose, grieving. The door opened and the flowers were brought in. Immediately, the atmosphere changed. I noticed, but did not remark on it; it was the others in the room who spoke first. I know I'm a florist and I am supposed to notice the difference flowers make, but I never realized what a fitting tribute to someone's life they can be. They comfort the grieving, and allow others to express their love and compassion. Ralph had always supported my ventures in life, but in death he had taught me his final lesson.

Tina M. Stoecker

Kath Bretherick, my florist friend in England, always tells customers that potted plants need proper care and nutrition to thrive. She and her staff once received a telephone call for help from a lady who complained about her cyclamen plant. She had been told to water it from the bottom but was still having great difficulty getting the water into the holes. Having turned the pot upside down, she was holding it under a running water tap. She was worried because the soil was washing out!

A Blooming Ring

At our flower shop, it would be a true statement to say that we get emotionally involved with our customers. We share all of the aspects of their lives, from birth to proms to weddings to death.

One young man started as a customer, became a delivery person, and then became a friend. So when it came time for him to propose to a young lady, we had to give him a few ideas.

Jim took Kara to a wonderful, quaint restaurant, well known locally for excellent food, great service, and a romantic atmosphere. They enjoyed a delicious dinner, and then their server delivered a beautiful red rose to their table, at which time Jim got down on his knee and presented the rose to his sweetheart. Nestled in the center of its fragile petals was a beautiful, sparkling, diamond ring.

Kara was, of course, overwhelmed. Surprised and crying, she quickly accepted, to the applause of the other patrons. After this most memorable proposal, Jim drove her by the large outdoor sign at our flower shop, which read, "Kara, we hope you said yes!"

Vonda LaFever

In the depths of winter I finally learned that within me there lay an invincible summer.

—Albert Camus

The Question

I am a floral designer. Along with owning a retail flower shop, as a floral commentator and instructional designer I have traveled across the country and into Canada teaching design skills. Often, people will ask how I came to be involved in this profession. I tell them that my part-time job in a flower shop during high school led me to a lifelong love of design as a process, with flowers as my medium. Over the years I have increased my design skills through independent study, by attending classes presented by international designers, and in the daily work experiences of design. As I have increased in skill and changed my level of job responsibilities, the oft-repeated story of my beginning interest in flowers and this industry has remained the same.

Recently, when speaking before a group, I was asked "the question." As I began my somewhat memorized spiel about how and why I became a floral designer, a moment from my childhood came back to me clearly. I stumbled over the words about how I had made this a career choice as I remembered a voice from my past. . . .

I dearly loved my first-grade teacher. You may have seen her. In her younger days, she had once read aloud to her students as Norman Rockwell sketched their picture in a one-room schoolhouse here in Georgia. As the story is told, Rockwell in his travels had been looking for such a rural schoolroom and someone had directed him to hers. When I gaze at a copy of the print that hangs on my office wall, the older teacher's face that I remember holds many more years of life experience. I was a student in her class at a newer school in the last year before her retirement. I remember her as a dedicated teacher who was also warm and encouraging.

Lost mid-answer for a moment in the dark recesses of my memory, I saw a wooden shelf with a small pottery vase on it. I remembered placing some fresh garden flowers—maybe small orange zinnias and yellow marigolds—into the vase. I felt myself spill a few drops as I poured in the water. I heard a woman's voice say, "There, that's pretty. I think you might arrange flowers when you grow up." I wondered during my speech if it had been my grandmother's voice, since she grew flowers in her garden as well, but later I recalled placing flowers in a small glass vase on the corner of the teacher's desk. I could clearly see the bright, sunny windows of my first-grade room. I vaguely remembered then that she had brought flowers from her yard, and I had enjoyed arranging them in her vases.

This brought to mind the real question. Did she, through her years of experience and wisdom, see a spark of interest and talent? Was I, a child having enjoyed special praise, being influenced toward the area of floral design? Or was it just coincidence that the memory returned as I explained my choice of professions? Apparently, arranging fresh flowers gave me pleasure then, as it does now. To have lingered in my memory, my teacher's notice of that fact must have touched my heart. As to other possible lasting effects, I realized that we as adults need to be ever mindful of the predictions we make to the listening ears of little ones. Sometimes, children live up to our expectations.

Sharon S. McGukin

To every thing there is a season, and a time for every purpose under heaven.

—*Ecclesiastes 3:1*

NONIE'S GARDEN

I've been in the floral industry for over twenty-eight years now, but when I look back, it really began over forty years ago and all because my grandma wanted a companion to help in the garden. My grandma, whom I fondly called Nonie, and my grandpa lived with our family from the day I was born. Nonie had the most beautiful flower garden, which took up most of our back, front, and side yards. Since my brother was too busy playing baseball or doing other things, flowers just weren't interesting to him. So when I was old enough to walk, as I've been told, Nonie would take me into her garden where I could do things that, at the time, held my interest and would do so for the rest of my life.

Nonie taught me exactly how to select flowers for planting, where to plant them, and how to care for and nurture them into beautiful blossoms. I remember those days vividly; when I sit back, I can smell the astilbe, filipendula, peonies, and all the other old-fashioned fragrances of her garden. She never worried that I would pull out a weed or a flower or if I mixed up the seeds; she just let me enjoy the beauty that we created.

When the garden was at its peak, we would select the best, most fragrant blooms, cut them, and bring them into the house to arrange in glass vases to place everywhere we could find space. Then, when we were finished, Nonie would make a fantastic meal for our family, as cooking was her second love.

I had no idea what an impact those very carefree days would have on my future. Today, I'm an international floral design instructor and speaker and can't ever imagine doing anything else. I have a beautiful flower garden that is planted in exactly the same way as I learned to do it so many years ago. I even have several of those same plants in my garden, which I've transplanted from house to house over all these years.

Nonie lived with me in her later years and gardened with me

until she passed away at the age of eighty. I wanted to use her garden as a design for her special memorial. I purchased hundreds of garden flowers from the florist, picked flowers from our garden, and got ready to design her funeral arrangements and casket spray at home in my kitchen because it seemed so personal. The side arrangements were huge and all done as if we had dug up her garden and placed it in the funeral home. When I got ready to design the casket spray, I realized that I had forgotten to purchase a container for the floral foam. As it was late in the evening, no florists were open. Since the funeral was the next morning, I searched the kitchen for a substitute container. Knowing our kitchen so well, Nonie must have been helping me because I found two aluminum turkey roasting pans that were large enough to completely recreate her garden across her entire casket. The funeral director still comments about "Nonie's garden" and how he has never seen another.

I really was blessed to have had a grandma like Nonie who unknowingly steered me into the great career of flowers. I never would have dreamed that the little boy playing in the garden would get to say thank you in such a personal way to his grandma, who I'm sure is still creating beautiful gardens that someday I'll again get to be a part of.

Kevin Ylvisaker

Flowers are restful to look at.
They have neither emotions nor conflicts.

—Sigmund Freud

Flower Small Talk

When my husband-to-be's father died two months before our wedding, I was honored to do the family's floral tributes. I had been in the floral industry my entire life, mostly as a designer and instructor of floral design. When designing the casket spray, I included several personal items as he was an avid ice fisherman. I used his special pole, lures, and a couple of hats—one with "Grandpa" on it, the other with some Minnesota fishermen's phrases I won't repeat here! It was a labor of love, for my fiancé and his family.

The design was delivered early, but when it arrived at the funeral home there were already many family members there. Previously, I had met some of this large extended family, so relatives approached me to compliment me on my design—its content, thoughtfulness, appropriateness—to the point where I was embarrassed. Because I was uncomfortable with all the attention paid to my flowers, I left the room.

When my fiancé, John, found me and heard why I had left the room, he explained, in his gentle way, that "the flowers are a bridge for the grief. Some of these people have not seen each other for months or years. They have nothing in common. The flowers are the comfortable connection that lead into a reintroduction."

This was a gentle reminder for me of the power of flowers, that they are able to bring peace and joy, and are an essential bridge for communication.

Ardith E. Beveridge

Royal Red

Of all the years that Bretherick's has been in business in England, one of the highlights was the year, in the early seventies, that we were selected to create the floral arrangements for a spectacular dinner honoring the visit of Princess Grace of Monoco.

It was specified that the designs should be predominately red and white and that we were to create a different design for each round dining table, several large arrangements to decorate the ballroom, and two more that would welcome guests in the entranceway.

We used dozens of red roses, red carnations, and bunches and bunches of trailing foliage and ferns. We really wanted the designs to be spectacular and unusual, so we tried to acquire proteas to use as the main focus of all the designs. Proteas are very unusual-looking flowers that dry beautifully and create a visually striking focal effect. These were not readily available from our local floral wholesaler, and the Dutch flower vendors hadn't started bringing flowers into the country as they do now. After many phone calls and numerous contacts, we were finally able to arrange to have them sent directly to us from Africa through a friend who lived there.

The motif used throughout the designs was cascading and interlocking rings. Flower clusters were designed at the top of each ring and a large, abundant display of flowers was created at the base.

Security was tight surrounding this event, and everyone from our shop had to go through security checks, be issued special name tags, and then be individually checked each and every time we carried something into or out of the area. Today we are used to this type of treatment; back then it was quite surprising and unusual.

We kept hoping to catch a glimpse of the princess—and maybe even have a word with her—but unfortunately we were whisked away before she arrived. When we returned to clean up, we were told that the princess had greatly admired the floral experience we had created and was extremely pleased with the unusual designs and the ambience of the room. The proteas were especially well received, and we found several missing from the designs during the cleanup. All in all, we were thrilled that we had created a sensation with the beauty and fragrance of flowers—and for such a special lady!

Kathleen Bretherick

In joy or sadness, flowers are our constant friends.
We eat, drink, sing, dance, and flirt with them.

—Kokuzo Okakura

No Flowers, Please

Flowers are very much a part of my life. Starting to work in a flower shop at the age of fourteen, I often saw the joy that flowers brought to someone's life. I feel that the most comfort flowers can provide is at the time of a death. Flowers sent to the home soon after a death tell the family that they are loved and that their loved one was well thought of, which gives the family a sense of peace. The flowers chosen by the family for the service are as personalized as the individuals themselves. Often, we incorporate a personal article or memento of the person so that the flowers become a vital part of the funeral or memorial service. They are a way for senders to express their grief and their sympathy, as well as for the family to feel comfort and love. Flowers have always been my expression of sympathy, and after attending a memorial service that by family request had not a single flower arrangement, I feel even more strongly that flowers need to be present at a funeral.

Recently, my cousin, age forty-two, died suddenly of a heart attack. At her request, her organs were donated to persons in need. She was no longer married, so her parents had the sad responsibility of her funeral arrangements. At first, they intended to do nothing. No memorial service, nothing. After a few days, I received a call telling me there would be a memorial service. Since it was to be out of state and I would not be able to attend, I picked up the phone and ordered flowers. Signing the card with my brother's and sister's names, I felt better. That was my way of grieving.

The next morning my dad phoned, specifically to tell me

that my aunt had requested no flowers. "Oh, well," I told my father, "there will be some there from us." He begged that we *please* honor her wishes. So I called the flower shop again, intending to cancel my order; instead, I changed the order. I asked her to deliver the flowers I had originally requested to the same place, for the same service, but with one important change: no card.

Florists are much like doctors in their respect for confidentiality. I felt better knowing that the loved ones who attended the memorial service could at least look at the flowers to help ease their pain. My mission was complete, or so I thought.

My mother called the next day to tell me that there was one beautiful floral arrangement at the service, but that the family did not know whom it had come from. It sat up front; and with all its natural beauty, it stood grandly, doing what flowers do best—bring feelings of hope, new life, and comfort. My mother said that something of beauty in a sad situation made her feel better. At the conclusion of that phone call, she said, "Thank you." Leaving it at that, we both understood.

Vonda LaFever

Yet no, not words, for they
But half can tell love's feeling;
Sweet flowers alone can say
What passion fears revealing.

—*Thomas Hood*

Delivering Happiness

Owning a small-town flower shop is both a challenge and a joy all its own. Often I have said to a returning delivery person, "Did you deliver happiness?," and the answer will detail some form of joy, surprise, or pleasure. Occasionally I will send out an unexpected delivery of my own to someone I have been thinking of that day. I enjoy sharing the flowers more than selling them, so it is a perk I give myself, usually without a lot of thought or planning.

Once, on a particularly beautiful and sunny fall day, I was thinking of someone in my church who was going through a divorce. I knew that she, the mother of three, was having a particularly hard time dealing with the loss of her long marriage. As my delivery person was leaving on her rounds, I asked her to deliver a small bundle of fresh flowers in vivid fall colors to this person. I had carefully wrapped them in cellophane and tied them with a cheerful raffia bow. I enclosed a small card indicating that I was thinking of her and that I had wanted to share the beauty of this fall day. Once the van pulled away, I promptly forgot about it in the hustle and bustle of daily business.

Months later, a customer came into the shop late one afternoon, all smiles. In her typically upbeat, positive way, she said, "I just wanted to stop by and give you a hug!" She is by nature a very happy and loving person, so I accepted her hug without surprise. Then, in a more serious tone, she told me that one day the previous fall she was having difficulty dealing with her impending divorce. As she lay on her bed thinking that she could not cope, she asked God to help her get up and get started again. Later the doorbell had rung and she had forced herself to answer it. "I opened the door to a pretty bouquet of fresh flowers, and as I read the card, I looked out and realized that it really *was* a beautiful day and that *life* was beautiful, too. It occurred to me then that my children needed me to be up for them now more than ever. Thank you for reminding me of that in such a special way!"

As I uttered a surprised "Oh, you're welcome!" I was caught off guard myself. I had totally forgotten that fall day, and only vaguely remembered sending the bundle of flowers. Suddenly I realized, as I had so many times before, that sending flowers to someone unexpectedly hadn't really been my idea. I was merely the person God had asked to deliver some needed bit of happiness.

Sharon S. McGukin

If I had 24 hours for living,
the things that don't matter could wait.
I'd play with the children and hear all their stories,
I'd tell you I love you, before it's too late.

—*Author unknown*

If we had only twenty-four hours left to our life, what would we do with them? We would probably choose to spend them with those we love. Use every day to tell others how much they mean to you. It's really easy and doesn't take much time to touch others in ways they don't expect. Tuck notes into a child's lunch bag. Lay a rose across a pillow at night; place a refreshing carnation on top of a plate at dinner. Flowers are one of life's small pleasures. Spirits are instantly lifted with the receipt of an unexpected bouquet of fresh flowers. Take a minute to show someone you care with a flower and a note—before it's too late.

Contributor Earned Designations

CPAE Speaker Hall of Fame

Established in 1977 by the National Speakers Association, the Council of Peers Award for Excellence (CPAE Speaker Hall of Fame) is a lifetime award for speaking excellence and professionalism given to speakers who have been evaluated by their peers and been judged to have mastered seven categories: material, style, experience, delivery, image, professionalism, and communication.

CSP

The Certified Speaking Professional designation, established in 1980 by the National Speakers Association, is the speaking industry's international measure of professional platform skill. In addition to their proven track record of continuing speaking experience and expertise, CSPs are committed to ongoing education, outstanding service, and ethical behavior. The CSP designation is conferred only on those accomplished speakers who have earned it by meeting strict criteria, including: serving at least 100 different clients within a 5-year period; presenting at least 250 professional speaking engagements within the same 5-year period; and submitting testimonial letters from clients served.

NSA

The National Speakers Association (NSA) is an international association of more than 3,800 members dedicated to advancing the art and value of experts who speak professionally. For more than 25 years, NSA has provided resources and education designed to enhance the business acumen and platform performance of professional speakers. Please visit NSA's Web site at www.nsaspeaker.org.
NSA: The Voice of the Speaking Profession.

AIFD

The American Institute of Floral Designers is the floral industry's leading nonprofit organization committed to establishing and maintaining higher standards in professional floral design. With nearly 1,000 members worldwide, AIFD and its members are in the forefront of the industry in presenting educational and design programs. Membership in AIFD is selective. To be accepted, a candidate must fulfill rigid qualifications and demonstrate advanced professional ability. Applicants must successfully complete a two-part process in which they prove their design abilities, first, through a portfolio of photographs, and then through an actual on-site design.

NDSF

National Diploma of the Society of Floristry in England

PFCI

Professional Floriculture Commentators International serves as an industry resource for floral commentators and educators. The PFCI designation signifies a dedication to excellence in floral commentary, leadership, knowledge, and a commitment to personal and industry growth.

AAF

American Acadamy of Floriculture is an honor that is achieved by individuals meeting the Acadamy's high standards of service to the industry and community.

P.Eng

Professional Engineer

TMF

Texas Master Florist

RD

Registered Dietician

LD

Licensed Dietician

CONTRIBUTORS

Dona Abbott is an artist living in Boulder, Colorado. She can be contacted through her website at <http://members.aol.com/dabbot.303>.

Her favorite flowers are the agapanthus and hydrangea.

Bill Aldrich has written about gardening for the *Chicago Tribune,* is editor of *Chicagoland Gardening* magazine, and has served as president of the Garden Writers Association of America.

His favorite flower is the phalaenopsis orchid.

Emory Austin, CSP, CPAE, is a dynamic, "pin-drop" professional speaker who works with organizations seeking more mission orientation and a stronger sense of purpose, profit, and vision throughout their ranks. She uses humor, skill, strategy building, and inspiration to shine new lights on themes such as leadership, change, and customer service. Contact her at 704-663-7575.

Her favorite flower is the rose.

Caprice Alicia Baker is a floral designer for the *Designs of the Times* florist shop in West Melbourne, Florida. However, her first passion is political writing. Caprice has three adult children and one beautiful granddaughter.

Her favorite flower is the Casablanca lily.

Kathy Baker is president of The Write Choice, a Kent, Ohio, based business-writing and editing company that specializes in public relations and marketing materials. She also gives presentations on a variety of humorous and inspirational topics to groups of all sizes. Contact her at 330-384-1311 or <kabaker@bright.net>.

Her favorite flower is the lilac.

Ginger Kean Berk is a professional consumer craft designer who is delighted to share her designs and love of fabric with many people through teaching and publications.

She loves any yellow flower, especially mums and daffodils.

Liz Bernstein is a wife and the mother of three daughters. While she loves to be surrounded by flowers inside and out of her home, the gardens she has created in her mind far surpass those she has created in her yard!

Her favorite flower is French lavender.

Ardith E. Beveridge, AAF, AIFD, PFCI, is the director of education at the Koehler & Dramm's Institute of Floristry in Minneapolis, Minnesota. She has been selected to design for some of America's most prestigious events, including being a lead floral designer for the Tournament of Roses Parade, and a presidential inauguration guest floral designer. Ardith presents seminars on a variety of topics, including design trends, color, and care and handling. She can be reached at 612-331-3307 or <ardithb@ix.netcom.com>.

Her favorite flower is the calla.

Dianna Booher is an author who has published thirty-five books, including *Communicate with Confidence!* (McGraw-Hill, 1994) and *Fresh-Cut Flowers for a Friend* (J. Countryman, 1997). Several have been major book club selections. She has been interviewed by *Good Morning America,* CNN, National Public Radio, *USA Today,* and *The Wall Street Journal.* Dallas-based Booher Consultants specializes in personal productivity, life balance, and communication—written, oral, interpersonal, gender. Contact her at 817-868-1200 or <dianna_booher@booherconsultants.com>.

Her favorite flower is the rose.

John O. Boyd III is president of Transformation Management, Inc. He works with organizations to improve customer and employee retention and align business processes with customer expectations. His "Just in Time Learning" approach enables organizations to build highly effective teams. Contact him at 800-639-8999 or <jboyd@transformation-mgt.com>. Also visit <www.transformation-mgt.com>.

His favorite flower is the jack-in-the-pulpit.

Kathleen Bretherick, NDSF, is a past president of The Society of Floristry in England. She has held the Society Diploma since 1957. A chief examiner and city and guilds assessor, she organizes flower demonstrations and shows, and has judged floristry throughout the country. Fifty years ago she established the firm of Brethericks, and now with her daughter and business partner, Sandra, they run two shops. She is the author of numerous books on floristry. She can be reached at 180 Harrogate Road, Leeds LS7 4NZ, West Yorkshire, England.

Her favorite flowers are the rubrum lily and the white gardenia.

Marilyn Rose Brosang, AIFD, TMF, AAF, is the main designer in their family business, Brosang's Flowers, in Tyler, Texas. She is presently a member of the AFS service team serving as a designer, instructor, and commentator. Marilyn is a wife and the mother of four children and one grandchild. Her interests include travel, golf, interior design, and gardening.

Her favorite flower is the rose.

Loretta Daum Byrne is an artist/designer/writer who has taken great delight in providing artwork and designs for everyone's "inner child." She focuses on ethnic peoples and their cultures and offers a catalog of over 100 of her works in the form of patterns, including several animal and fantasy creatures. Send $3.00 to Little Lotus, P.O. Box 105, Cambridge, Wisconsin 53523 for a catalog.

Her favorite flower is the pink lotus.

Peter V. Cannice was born in Schenectady, New York. He currently serves on numerous humanitarian and community service boards and is the community elected co-chairman for the Center for Disease Control HIV Prevention Planning Group for the state of Iowa. Peter will always be known for his commitment to justice, especially justice for the emotionally and physically disabled. He is an acknowledged speaker, actor, and model. Feel free to contact him at his home, 1011 Day Street, Des Moines, Iowa 50314 or <Peter50314@aol.com>.

His favorite flower is the azalea.

Arnold "Nick" Carter is vice president of communications research for the Nightingale-Conant Corporation. He served for six years in the U.S. Navy and is a retired Lieutenant Commander, USNR. Since working at Nightingale-Conant, Nick has had three books published and has produced many albums on cassette. He has twice received the prestigious George Washington Honor Medal from the Freedom Foundation for his essays on democracy and the free-enterprise system.

His favorite flower is the rose.

David L. Coake is a former retail flower shop owner, and is editor-in-chief of *Florists' Review,* the floral industry's oldest and largest trade publication.

His favorite flower is the hyacinth.

Rona Coleman, NDSF, grew up in England where she co-directed a garden center in London, England, with her husband, Stanley, for many years. She was the first British florist to be inducted into the American Institute of Floral Designers. She founded and directed the school of floristry, Flower Design of Britain, in England, and has a teaching studio in Nagoya, Japan. She has authored numerous books and has taught around the world. She is currently living in Missouri. For information regarding Flower Design of Britain, contact Rona via fax at 660-646-0745, or <jhelmer@greenhills.net>. For information on courses in Britain visit <www.tama.or.jp/~fdb/index-e.htm>.

Her favorite flower is the daffodil.

Jacquelin H. Dannemiller, AIFD, is an agricultural education instructor at Career Enrichment Park in Westminster, Colorado. She is active in Teleflora and the American Institute of Floral Designers as an educator and a lecturer. Contact her at 303-428-2600, ext. 5233 or <ndannemi@xplorenet.com>.

Her favorite flower is the dendrobian orchid.

Tony DeMasi, of Deptford, New Jersey, is the editor-in-chief/co-publisher of *Giftware News,* a trade magazine for the gift industry. He is also the author of the best-selling book *Your Wedding . . . Perfectly Planned* (Friedman Group, 1992). Married for twenty-five years and the father of two, he enjoys gardening as a sport, explaining, "Sometimes you win, sometimes you lose. The challenge of getting things to grow is fun."

His favorite flower is the rubrum lily.

Lois DiGiacomo of North Canton, Ohio, is the founder/director of Rainbow Repertory Company, a traveling theater company. She is a playwright, freelance writer, drama teacher, speaker, and seminar leader. Lois can assist business, social service, education, and law communities to use drama creatively in communication and training. Contact her at 330-966-9440 or <loisrrc@juno.com>.

Her favorite flower is the rose.

Amy Doggett-Burns lives with her husband, Dennis, in Cleveland, Ohio. Amy has traveled extensively throughout the United States and Europe for both business and leisure. She enjoys art and music, and spends her free time sewing, gardening, and traveling. Amy is a 1993 graduate of The Ohio State University and is a member of Alpha Omicron Pi, Cleveland West Alumni.

Her favorite flower is the pansy.

Frances Dudley is the publisher of *Florists Review Magazine,* the largest and most influential publication for professional florists. The company also publishes books on floral-related topics. For a copy of its catalog, fax a request to 785-266-0333.

Her favorite flowers are old-fashioned garden flowers.

Betsy Edwards, CCD, CPD, of Hollis, New Hampshire, is a freelance designer, writer, and speaker in the craft and decorative painting industry. She and her husband have four grown children, five grandchildren, and two cats. Contact her at 603-465-3193 or <justbetsys@aol.com>.

Her favorite flower is the blue bonnet.

Poul Einshøj and his wife, Karen, have worked with flowers and floristry for more than thirty years, Karen as a florist, Poul with Smithers-Oasis, a major manufacturer and supplier of floral foam and accessories for the floral industry. They are Danish and have lived and worked with their family in Germany, and are now settled in Great Britain.

His favorite flower is the tulip.

Henry Ford is a public speaker, trainer, and author of *Success Is You* (Kendall/Hunt, 1995) and *The Power of Association* (Kendall/Hunt, 1996). A graduate of the Les Brown Speaking for a Living Workshop and a member of the National Speakers Association, Henry shares his messages with audiences around the world. Henry may be contacted at 330-425-8776 or <success_is_you@ameritech.net>. Also visit him at <www. success_is_you.com>.

His favorite flower is the tulip.

Gail Fletcher-Cooke lives on the beautiful Isle of Man, an unspoiled part of Europe. It is often said that to visit the island is like stepping back in time. Wild orchids grow among the steam trains and trams. Gail is president of Craftime Ltd., the United Kingdom's largest distributor of craft dolls and patterns, a company she started in 1989. She can be reached by fax at 011-44-1624-817820, or <CraftimeUK@aol.com>.

Her favorite flower is an English rose.

Barbara Glanz, CSP, is an internationally known professional speaker who works with organizations that want to improve morale, and people who want to rediscover the joy in their work and in their lives. She is the author of *CARE Packages for the Home—Dozens of Ways to Regenerate Spirit Where You Live* (Andrews McNeal, 1998), and her topic areas include "Regenerating Spirit in the Workplace and in the Home" and "Building Customer Loyalty." Contact her at 708-246-8594 or <www. barbaraglanz.com>.

Her favorite flower is the gardenia.

Leslie Hartsock, of Bartlesville, Oklahoma, is a wife and the mother of seven children. She directed a children's musical performing group for thirteen years and currently designs children's crafts, published in national magazines. She can be contacted at <DLHARTS@aol.com>.

Her favorite flower is the bleeding heart.

Priscilla Hauser is America's "First Lady of Decorative Painting" and with love and enthusiasm has been teaching the joys of painting for almost four decades. Priscilla's studio is located on the white sands of the Gulf of Mexico between Panama City Beach and Destin. There, students come from all over the world to learn to paint and to teach. She is the author of many books and a guest on many TV craft shows. Contact her at P.O. Box 521013, Tulsa, Oklahoma 74152-1013 or at 918-743-6072 or <PHauser376@aol.com>. Also visit <www.priscilla hauser.com>.

Her favorite flower is the rose.

Sharon L. Hetzel is founder and president of POWERnetwork, a training company with a soul that brings spirit into your personal life, your workplace, and your community. Their Lifeworks program includes a balanced menu of keynote presentations and/or course offerings. Contact her at 937-298-6620 or <powernetwork@earthlink.net>.

Her favorite flower is the tulip.

Liz Curtis Higgs, CSP, CPAE, is an award-winning speaker and the author of thirteen books—eight books of humor for women and five inspiring children's books, including *Bad Girls of the Bible and What We Can Learn from Them* (Water Brook Press, 1999), and *Mixed Signals* (Multnomah Publishers, 1999). For her free newsletter, "The Laughing Heart"®, call 800-762-6565.

Her favorite flower is freesia.

Dr. Kenneth H. Killen, CPM, of Rocky River, Ohio, has been a professional speaker for over 30 years. Ken has written more than 160 articles and 4 books, including *Managing Purchasing* (Irwin, 1995). He is the recipient of the J. Shipman Gold Medal, NAPM's (National Association of Purchasing Management) highest award. He specializes in buyer/seller negotiations training. He can be reached at 800-685-1219.

His favorite flower is the red carnation.

Pat Klima manages an information technology department for a major manufacturing firm. Her husband, Dennis, is a consultant in information services. Both are avid parents and golfers.

Her favorite flower is the orchid.

Ruth Kuhnle is a mother, grandmother, and great-grandmother. She has been a secretary, a craft shop owner, and a volunteer in a hospital gift shop.

Her favorite flower is the peace rose.

Tom Kumpf of Boulder, Colorado, is a Viet Nam veteran and an award-winning photographer who has traveled extensively and worked with Russian veterans of the war in Afghanistan and others suffering from PTSD (post-traumatic stress disorder), including children in Northern Ireland. He is the author/photographer of *Children of Belfast: Reclaiming Their Place Among the Stones* (Devenish Press, 1999). Visit him at <www.tomkumpf.com>.

His favorite flower is the bitterroot (lewisia rediviva pursh).

Elizabeth Jeffries, CSP, CPAE, works with organizations that want to put their mission into action and with people who want to get more meaning from their work. She is the author of *The Heart of Leadership: How to Inspire, Encourage and Motivate People to Follow You* (Kendall/Hunt, 1996). An award-winning speaker, Elizabeth can be reached in Louisville, Kentucky, at 502-339-1600 or <EJeffries@compuserve.com>. Also visit <www.tweed jeffries.com>.

Her favorite flower is the rose.

Vonda LaFever, AIFD, and her husband, Bud, own and operate a flower shop in Dixon, Illinois. She is a proud mother of three and a member of the American Institute of Floral Designers. You can contact her at <flowers@cin.net>.

Her favorite flower is the king protea.

Kathie LaForce, CMP, is the owner of Kathie's Creative Services, a floral preservation and event-planning company. She holds an MBA in international marketing and is a certified meeting planner. She is past president of the International Freeze Dry Floral Association and frequently writes columns for several national floral publications. Contact her at 650-573-0631 or <kcreate@slip.net>.

Her favorite flower is the rose.

Jim Lamancusa is currently attending the University of Colorado and is majoring in marketing and information systems. He is the author of *Dynamite Crafts for Special Occasions* (McGraw/Hill, 1993). He brings flowers on every one of his dates!

His favorite flower is the lilac.

Joe Lamancusa is the husband of the author of this book. Along with being the business manager of Kathy's speaking career, he is the owner of Visual Design Concepts, an advertising, marketing, and consulting business with clients in the floral, craft, and creative industries. He is also the president of Creative Directions, Inc., a company through which readers can order additional books and videos by Kathy Lamancusa. Contact him at 330-494-7224 or <joe@lamancusa.com>. Also visit <www.lamancusa.com>.

His favorite flower is the iris.

Joe Lamancusa Jr. is an explorer. A 2000 graduate of Miami University in Oxford, Ohio, his major is preparing him for a life as a manager in corporate America. However, he thinks this might not be very stimulating or exciting, so he sees himself perhaps teaching English in Nepal or studying rain forests in Australia. Joe feels the only things in life one regrets are the risks one doesn't take. He is the author of *Kid Cash: Creative Money Making Ideas* (McGraw Hill, 1993).

He loves all types of fragrant flowers.

Josephine (Jo) Lamancusa has four children and six grandchildren. She is a teacher of tole and decorative painting and does oil paintings and watercolors. She is a resident of Twinsburg, Ohio.

Her favorite flower is the lilac.

Mrs. Nguyen Ngoc Lan, AIFD, BSc., DTCM, is the founder and director of the International Florist Academy School. She holds degrees in chemical engineering, traditional Chinese medicine, and naturotherapy from Japan. She is a respected floral designer, teacher, and commentator. She is the author of three floral art books and is presently working on her new book, an in-depth study of Floratherapy. Contact her at 5475 Victoria Avenue, Montreal, Quebec, Canada, H3W 2P7 or 514-739-7152.

Her favorite flower is cattleya orchid.

Eric Larsen lives in the middle Tennessee area. For the past twenty-five years he has worked for a major construction equipment dealer. He enjoys meeting people from all over the world, collects the music and memorabilia of Julio Iglesias, and loves good old-fashioned quiet time at home.

He loves commercial white roses, home-grown daffodils, and the blue lupines that naturally grow wild and cover the hills in California.

Geraldine Adamich Laufer is an Atlanta horticulturist and floral poet. She is the author of the award-winning book *Tussie-Mussies* (Workman, $22.95). A captivating public speaker, Geri's media appearances include ABC's *Good Morning America, Home Matters* on the Discovery Channel, and *Between the Lines* on TBS and Minnesota Public Radio, along with the major U.S. flower shows. Contact her at 770-642-0330 or <GeriL@ufer.com> to schedule an appearance.

Her favorite flowers include coral roses and trillium.

Chuck Levine teaches horticulture at Hennepin Technical College in Brooklyn Park, Minnesota. He is an avid gardener whose garden is often featured on garden tours. He is available for speaking engagements and to lead garden tours. He can be contacted at 651-487-5906 or <levi0052@tc.umn.edu>.

His favorite flower is the gardenia.

Celeste Lilly-Rossman, AIFD, has worked in the professional floral field for nineteen years. She was inducted into the American Institute of Floral Designers in 1991. Along with her husband, Tom, she is raising two sons on a northwestern Ohio farm. Creative writing and photography are her pastimes.

Her favorite flower is the lily.

Debi Linker of Morro Bay, California, and Lake City, Colorado, is a product designer, business teacher, and consultant for the creative industries. She specializes in helping small retailers become better managers of their business assets. Contact her at 805-772-3036 or <dlinker@creativebeginnings.com>.

Her favorite flower is the rose.

Florence Littauer, CSP, CPAE, is a dynamic professional speaker and best-selling author of more than twenty-seven books, with *Personality Plus* (Fleming H. Revell Publishers, 1983, 1992) selling over one million copies worldwide. As a well-known motivational and inspirational speaker, she speaks to over sixty diverse groups each year. Florence is one of a handful of women in the United States to be chosen for the Speakers Hall of Fame by the National Speakers Association and has a doctorate in humanities from Southwestern Adventist University. Contact her at 760-471-0233 or <CLASSSpkr@aol.com>. Also visit <www.CLASServices.com>.

Her favorite flower is the geranium.

Theresa Loe is a freelance writer and speaker specializing in herb/flower gardening, Victorian history, and cooking/home entertaining from the garden. Her work focuses on bringing the flavors and fragrances of the garden indoors through food and decoration. She is the author of *The Herbal Home Companion* (Kensington Publication Corp., 1996), and has produced two videos on garden entertaining. Contact her at Country Thyme Productions, P.O. Box 3090, El Segundo, California 90245, 310-322-6026 or 310-322-5946 (her fax) or <nothyme@aol.com>.

Her favorite flower is the sweet pea.

Eileen McDargh, CSP, CPAE, is a California-based professional speaker and "human capitalist." Author of *Work for a Living & Still Be Free to Live* (BookPartners, orig. 1985, revised 1998), she has spent more than two decades helping companies and individuals look at ways to create environments in which people thrive. Call her at 949-496-8640 or visit her website, <www.eileenmcdargh.com>.

Her favorite flower is the double-delight rose.

Sharon S. McGukin, AIFD, PCFI, is a designer, commentator, and instructor of floral design. She travels across the United States and Canada speaking to groups and participating in design forums. She has been featured in floral industry-related magazines. Sharon and her husband, Tim, reside in Carrollton, Georgia, and have three children.

Her favorite flower is the saracena.

Sharon McVary of Spring Lake Park, Minnesota, spent a number of years teaching high school business and English classes and operating a floral/gift shop before joining the ranks of nontraditional students to earn a theology degree. She currently serves as a senior high youth minister and confirmation coordinator.

Her favorite flower is the peony.

Kevin Michalowski is a book editor and a freelance writer/photographer. He specializes in natural subjects and the outdoors, including the place that hunting and fishing have in society. He can be reached at <michalowskik@krause.com>.

His favorite flower is the rose.

Hope Mihalap, CPAE, is a humorist and public radio personality. She is the winner of the Mark Twain Award for Humor and the Speaker Hall of Fame Award from the National Speakers Association. She is also a wife and the mother of three grown children and a better cook than she is a gardener, alas! Hope can be reached at 757-640-0333.

Her favorite flower is the lily of the valley.

Richard L. Milteer, AAF, AIFD, PFCI, TMF, is an internationally renowned floral industry consultant, motivational speaker, commentator, and historian. He is the president of Richmil, Inc., an industry-consulting firm providing operational guidance to commercial, industrial, and organizational floral groups around the globe. He can be reached at 612-937-7616 or <Richmil@worldnet.att.net>.

His favorite flower is the calla lily.

Patsy DeBernardis Moreland is a fiber artist living in Portland, Oregon. She has taught and exhibited locally. Her work has been published in national needlework and craft magazines. FIBERWORKS NW is her tour company specializing in escorted craft and scenic travel in the Pacific Northwest and Great Britain. She can be reached at 503-760-1816.

Her favorite flower is the rose.

Eleanor A. Morgan is a wife, mother, and retired RN. She has two grown children. While she and her husband enjoy gardening, her first love is cooking, a talent she inherited from her beloved grandmother.

Her favorite flower is the white carnation.

Sylvia P. Nichols, AIFD, opened The Window Box Florist in Cheshire, Connecticut, in 1977. A frequent speaker on floral topics, she is noted for her inspiring and often humorous presentations. She can be contacted at 800-723-1697.

Her favorite flower is the gardenia.

Libbey Oliver, a floral consultant, was honored in 1994 as flower arranger of the year by the American Horticultural Society. Through her business, Flowers & Gardens, she presents demonstrations across the country and has authored two books for Colonial Williamsburg on Christmas decoration. For over twenty years, Libbey managed the floral and Christmas decorations for Colonial Williamsburg. Contact her at 757-220-4632.

Her favorite flower is the cardinal flower
(lobelia cardinalis).

Allison Lynn Ondrey is a student at Penn State University, studying marketing and international business. She has a tattoo of a calla lily on her lower right back. This is also her mother's favorite flower. She would like to thank her first- and seventh-grade teacher, Mrs. Ravasio, for always believing in her.

Her favorite flower is the calla lily.

Jody Ondrus is a floral/craft designer and instructor. Her specialties are silk and dried florals and paper quilling. She is a member of the Society of Craft Designers and an American representative of the Quilling Guild of England. Her designs have been published in many craft magazines and are featured in *The Book of Quilling* by Malinda Johnston (Altamont Press, 1994, Sterling Publishing, Co., 1995).

Her favorite flower is the carnation.

Marion Stirrup Owen of Kodiak, Alaska, teaches organic gardening at the University of Alaska. A professional photographer, Marion is also president of Plantamins, Inc., the company that developed PlanTea, the organic tea bag fertilizer. She markets it worldwide from her Alaska office. She can be contacted at 907-485-5079 or <marion@ptialaska.net>. Also visit <www.plantea.com>.

Her favorite flower is the calendula.

Sharon Oxley of Sonora, California, owns a gift shop, Victoria Rose. She and her husband, Jim, live in a Victorian farmhouse with their two collies, four cats, and fourteen birds. Their home is filled with rose motif wallpaper, rose floral designs, and rose linens.

Her favorite flower is the rose.

Jim Pancero, CSP, CPAE, is a sales and sales management corporate consultant from Cincinnati, Ohio, and has never planted anything that lived for more than a few days.

His favorite flower is the rose.

Alan K. Parkhurst, AIFD, PFCI, was a flower shop owner for twenty-three years. He was educated in the United States and abroad and for twenty years has designed, competed, and judged in numerous U.S. design competitions. His work has been seen in *Professional Floral Designer* and *Florist's Review* magazines and he has written articles for the *Society of American Florists* magazine. He is currently the national floral design manager for Joann Stores, Inc.

His favorite flower is the iris.

Terry Paulson, Ph.D., CSP, CPAE, of Agoura Hills, California, is the 1998/99 president of the National Speakers Association and the author of *They Shoot Managers Don't They?* (Ten Speed Press, 1991), and *50 Tips for Speaking Like a Pro* (Crisp Publications, 1999). As a speaker, he helps leaders and teams make change work. Contact him at 818-991-5110 or <DrTerryP@aol.com>. Also visit <www.changecentral.com>.

His favorite flower is the daffodil.

Euneata Payne is a professional trainer and speaker living in Columbus, Ohio. Her mission is to help people succeed at work by overcoming challenges, building on their strengths, and developing superior communication skills. She can be contacted at 614-475-7904 or <imagemakerstraining@pobox.com>.

Her favorite flower is the rose.

Sue Pistone is the owner of Sue Pistone & Associates, a personal and professional development firm. As a professional speaker, Sue helps others to have more balance in their daily lives, gain a few extra hours each day, and experience less stress through her organization, time management, and personal and professional development seminars. For positive results, contact her at 800-409-ICAN (4226) or <SuePistone@aol.com>.

Her favorite flower is a pink rose.

Rocky Pollitz, AIFD, AAF, PFCI, CMG, is the Teleflora vice president of industry relations and the publisher of *Flowers & Magazine*. By special invitation, she taught at the Tokyo Flower Center in Japan and was a guest instructor of design at Teleflower in Sydney, Australia. She represented the United States at the International Design Show in Mexico City. Her expertise has been tapped by the White House, the Smithsonian Institute, Fiesta Floats in conjunction with the Rose Parade, the Franklin Mint, and the Los Angeles County Museum of Art.

Her favorite flower is the ranunculus.

Nido Qubein, CSP, CPAE, is past president of the National Speakers Association, a speaker, and the chairman of an international consulting firm. He has received many honors, including the Ellis Island Congressional Medal of Honor and the Cavett Award. He has written numerous books and has recorded scores of audio and video learning programs. You can reach Nido at Creative Services, Inc., P.O. Box 6008, High Point, North Carolina 27262-6008, 800-989-3010 or <NidoQ@aol.com>.

His favorite flower is the rose.

Terri Quillen is a "semiretired" registered nurse, writer, and crafts designer who is serving the Lord full-time through discipleship and the ministry of intercession. If you have a prayer need, or would like to share how God has touched your life, please write to Terri. Send letters to Terri Quillen/Q.C.C., 3100 Meridian Parke Drive, STE N-161, Greenwood, Indiana 46142.

Her favorite flower is the sweetheart rose.

Michael A. Raburn, AIFD, has been in the floral business for most of his adult life, currently as a design manager in Atlanta, Georgia. He was inducted into the American Institute of Floral Designers in 1989. He is the doting father of his daughter, Alex.

His favorite flower is the peony.

Naomi Rhode, CSP, CPAE, Speaker Hall of Fame, past president of the National Speakers Association, and 1997 winner of the Cavett Award, this organization's highest award. Author of *More Beautiful Than Diamonds—The Gift of Friendship* (Thomas Nelson Publishing, 1991), and *The Gift of Family—A Legacy of Love* (Thomas Nelson Publishing, 1991), plus coauthor and contributor for numerous books and publications, she is renowned for her ability to inspire an audience; she speaks to health care associations and corporate audiences. Naomi shares her expertise on leadership, team building, interpersonal communications, and relationships, plus motivation. Contact her at 602-225-9090 or <nrhode@smarthealth.com>.

Her favorite flower is the Lincoln rose.

Dr. Stephen Rittner is director of The Rittner's School of Floral Design in Boston, Massachusetts. His school attracts students from all over the United States and overseas. Contact him at 617-267-3824 or <stevrt@tiac.net>. Visit Rittner's School of Floral Design at <www.floralschool.com>.

His favorite flower: One is not enough!

Rosemarie Rossetti, Ph.D., is a professional speaker, trainer, consultant, and author. She works with people who want to feel at ease in front of a group and organizations that want their people to communicate more clearly. She gives keynote presentations to teach people how to deal with change, adversity and setbacks. As an interior horticulturist, she is coauthor of *The Healthy Indoor Plant* (Rosewell Publishing, 1992). She resides in Columbus, Ohio, and can be reached at <RRossetti@aol.com>.

Her favorite flower is the phalaenopsis orchid.

Sara Rowekamp of Cincinnati, Ohio, specializes in garden writing and speaking to gardeners of all ages and experience. She invites you to discover the newest plants for your garden in her book *New Varieties to Know and Grow* (Oak Leaf Publications), published bi-annually. Her written work has also been published in *National Gardening Magazine,* and her presentations have been enjoyed at various garden clubs and organizations in the Cincinnati area. She may be contacted at 513-347-3180 or at <oakleafpub@aol.com>.

Her favorite flower is the gardenia.

Lonni Miller Ryan works for a New York City public relations firm. She and her husband, Bill, live in Wayne, New Jersey, with their orange tabby cat, Francis.

Her favorite flower is the rose.

Carol Scherm is a wife, the mother of four, and the grandmother of five. She retired from the floral industry but donates her time and talent to nonprofit local organizations. She can be contacted at <Granma142@aol.com>.

Her favorite flower is the sterling rose.

Lynnette Schuepbach is the author of *Creative Woodcarving: Inspired by Nature* (Walnut Hollow, 1999), a woodcarving design book based on one of her poems. She is a certified picture framer, an educator, a massage therapist, and a nature enthusiast. She is the mother of two sons and currently works as assistant show director for Art Buyers Caravan trade shows. Contact her at 618-288-1598 or <lls@empowering.com>.

Her favorite flower is the daffodil.

Jim Somppi is co-owner and founder of The White Rose Custom Floral Design in Albany, Oregon. His interest in flowers began at an early age in his father's garden, and in the truest sense, Jim has turned his avocation into his vocation. The White Rose has been in business for fifteen years. He can be contacted at 541-924-9697.

His favorite flower is the white rose.

Tina M. Stoecker, AIFD, of Melbourne, Florida, is the 1998/99 president of the southern region of the American Institute of Floral Designers. Her floral artistry has appeared in *Florist, Florists' Review, Flowers&*, and on the cover of *Floral Management*. As a speaker, she has traveled the United States and Europe teaching and demonstrating creative floral design concepts. She can be contacted at 407-676-2452.

Her favorite flower is the lilac.

Penny E. Stone is a wife and the mother of three. She is a freelance writer with over 1,200 articles published. She is the author of *365 Easy and Affordable Dinner Menus That Even the Kids Will Love* (Champion Press, 1999). Penny can be contacted at <penworks@netusa1.net>.

Her favorite flower is the daisy.

Shea Szachara is Director of Creative and Educational Services for Delta Technical Coatings, Inc. based in Whittier, California. She has been a designer, author, and instructor in the creative industries for more than twenty years and maintains her home/office in Binghamton, New York. Her story "Neighborly Tulips" is written in memory of her mother, Florence Allen.

Her favorite flower is the moss rose.

Bryan Townsend, CSP, CPAE, of Talladega, Alabama, is a professional speaker and writer. He is the author of *Life Is an Adventure* (1995), and the coauthor of *Selling in the Bear Woods* (1998). As a speaker, he helps corporations and associations orchestrate successful meetings with humorous presentations on interpersonal relationships, teamwork, and customer service. Contact him at 205-763-7247 or <BryanTspkr@aol.com>. Also visit <www.dwd.net/townsend>.

His favorite flower is the carpet rose.

Kathy Tridente is the founder of KT Communications, a women-owned public relations/advertising firm in Newark, Delaware, serving myriad clients—from *Fortune* 500 companies to entrepreneurial firms across the United States. She can be contacted at 302-234-1119 or <ktridente@yahoo.com>.

Her favorite flower is the gardenia.

Betty Valle has been an author and a designer in the craft industry for twenty-eight years. She has written numerous magazine columns and instruction books, some pertaining to silk flower arranging. Her most recent article is "Grandma Bebe's Party Time" in *Pack-O-Fun* magazine. Now semiretired, she works in a local flower shop and also volunteers her talents to the hospital craft guild and programs for the senior center.

Her favorite flower is the lily of the valley.

Mike Vance is the author of the bestselling book *Think Out of the Box* (Career Press, 1995), and is the chairman of the Creative Thinking Association of America. He was the original dean of

Disney University. To book him for speaking engagements, call 800-445-6677. Lisa Wolf is Mike's administrative assistant.

Mike's favorite flower is the red rose.
Lisa's is the Sonia rose.

Al Walker, CSP, CPAE, of Columbia, South Carolina, is a professional speaker and a senior partner in Capital Training Group. He is known as "a big man with a big message," and whether he is leading a workshop for a dozen people or speaking to two thousand people at a convention, his love of life and his ability to help others see the humor in life always leave his audience wanting more. Contact him at 800-255-1982 or <walkeral@aol.com>.

His favorite flower is the magnolia.

Ronald Wallace is an international sales and marketing executive living in northwest New Jersey. Ron is married, with two adult children who were both born in the United Kingdom. He and his family emigrated to the United States in 1983.

His favorite flower is the carnation.

Allen D. Walters is a professional speaker who has delivered hundreds of motivational speeches and has conducted teamwork and leadership seminars across America. He is the author of *Then & Now, a Vietnam Veteran's Journey* (1997). Al's passion is speaking to teenagers on leadership, democracy, and responsibility. He can be contacted at 419-884-2113 or <Allen@thecheckers.com>. Also visit <www.thecheckers.com>.

His favorite flower is the sunflower.

Susan E. Warkentin, P.Eng., is a professional mechanical engineer with subsequent diplomas in fashion design and education. After various positions in the manufacturing sector, she can now be found each day in front of a high school mathematics class. She resides in Owen Sound, Ontario, Canada, with her husband, two active young children, and the family cat. She takes refuge from the daily insanity in humor, gardening, sewing, and watercoloring.

Her favorite flower is the alstroemeria.

Alison E. Webb, AIFD, is a professional retail florist who has been working with flowers for over twenty-five years. She works for the Rutland Beard Florist of Ruxton, Maryland, just outside Baltimore, and can be contacted at 410-321-1737.

She loves all types of flowers.

Michael Webb is editor of *The RoMANtic Newsletter: Hundreds of Fun and Creative Tips to Enrich Your Relationship* (Hyperion, 2000), and the author of *The RoMANtic's Guide.* He is widely regarded as a romance expert and gives hundreds of radio and TV interviews each year. Contact him at 888-4ROMANTIC or visit <www.TheRomantic.com>.

His favorite flower is the peony.

Louise G. Weder is an eighty-five-year-old mother of five, grandmother of eight, great-grandmother of two, and continues to be active in the wholesale floral industry. Though she is on the board of directors of nine companies in five different states, she is best known for good deeds outside her home each day. Widow of Erwin Weder, founder of Highland Supply Corporation, she has also been involved as vice president and in the administration, design, customer service, sales, productions, and shipping aspects of the business.

Her favorite flower is the yellow rose.
Her husband, Erwin, always called her his yellow rose of Texas.

Chandra Wilfong is a wife and a real estate assistant living in Phoenix, Arizona. She enjoys hiking, diving, and traveling.

Her favorite flower is the daffodil.

Julie Wilkinson, AIFD, PFCI, AAF, has been involved in the floral industry as a marketer, educator, and speaker for over thirty years. Ms. Wilkinson's expertise has been an influence throughout the United States, as well as in over a dozen foreign countries. Ms. Wilkinson can be contacted at 618-692-1688.

Her favorite flower is the garden rose.

Ann Pettingell Wilton is a garden writer, photographer, and illustrator. Ann founded Aspen's first garden club, The Pardon My Garden Club, in 1993. She has written and edited the club's award-winning newsletter for the past six years. Ann writes for newspapers, magazines, and is working on a book called *Humor in the Garden.* She is a member of Garden Writers Association of America (GWAA) and American Society of Media Photographers (ASMP). She can be contacted at <wilton@rof.net>.

Her favorite flower is
". . . whatever flower is in front of my nose,
love the one you're with."

Barb Wingfield, from Rushsylvania, Ohio, is a speaker and the author of the book *Reasons to Say WOW!!!, A Celebration of Life's Simple Pleasures* (Web Publishing, 1995). Her company, Morale Builders, specializes in helping organizations add praise and recognition. She is married, the mother of three, the mother-in-law of one, and an aunt of eleven. She can be contacted at 800-276-0101 or <bewingfiel@aol.com>.

Her favorite flower is the red rose.

Kathy G. Wise, RD, LD, of North Canton, Ohio, is president of Wise Nutrition Concepts, Inc., and editor of the newsletter *Wise Concepts: Quick, Convenient & Healthy Ideas for Busy People.* As a registered dietitian and a speaker, she works with companies and individuals, providing nutrition and wellness programs to optimize their health goals. Contact her at 330-497-1882. Also visit <www.anutritionchoice.com>.

Her favorite flower is the yellow peace rose.

Toni Wood is a journalist and writer living in Shawnee, Kansas. She writes for magazines and newspapers, including *The Kansas City Star.* She and her husband have three boys. Contact her at 913-441-0659 or <toniwrites@aol.com>.

Her favorite flower is the iris.

Kevin Ylvisaker, AIFD, PFCI, of Mukwonago, Wisconsin, is past president of the American Institute of Floral Designers. He is a freelance floral designer who has worked on designs for presidential inaugurations, the Tournament of Roses Parade, and in many international schools. Contact him at 414-363-1199 or <kylvisak@execpc.com>.

His favorite flower is the cosmos.

Zig Ziglar has been happily married to Jean Abernathy for fifty-three years and has four children and four grandchildren. He became a born-again Christian on July 4, 1972, and has been a Sunday school teacher for seventeen years. He is the author of fifteen books, including nine best-sellers. Zig is chairman of the board of The Zig Ziglar Corporation and gives presentations to audiences around the world. He can be reached at 972-233-9191.

His favorite flower is the rose.

More Flower Stories?

What flowers bring back fond memories for you? Is there a time in your life when flowers brought you joy, gave you a hug, or helped you send a message to someone you love? I would love to hear your special story. I am planning future books using a similar format, which will feature stories that illustrate the profound effect flowers have on life, celebrations, love, romance, passion, and sorrow. I am seeking heartwarming stories, reflections, and memories of up to three pages in length to include in these volumes. I am also very interested in including little-known information about the care and handling of flowers, tips for surrounding yourself with flowers, and garden advice.

I invite you to join me in these future projects by sending your stories and information for special consideration. If selected for inclusion, you will be listed as a contributor and may include a biographical paragraph. Send your submissions to:

CREATIVE DIRECTIONS, INC.
FLORAL MEMORIES
8755 Cleveland Avenue
North Canton, OH 44720

You can also submit by E-mail to
<info@lamancusa.com>.

"Friday's Flowers" E-mail Newsletter

If you want to be touched by more stories, memories, tips, and ideas related to flowers, subscribe to our FREE E-mail newsletter "FRIDAY'S FLOWERS." Each Friday you will receive a snippet of floral information or short story about flowers directly on your desktop. It will get you ready for the weekend! To enroll, send a "subscribe *Friday's Flowers*" message to <info@lamancusa.com>.

LAMANCUSA *LIVE!*

Kathy's live motivational or business presentation of *Flowers Are Forever* would be a perfect addition to your next convention or conference. For presentation information, check her website <www.lamancusa.com>, E-mail <info@lamancusa.com>, or call 330-494-7224.

About the Author

Kathy Lamancusa, *"The Creative Trend Strategist,"* is a professional speaker, an author, a floral designer, a television host, and a gardener. She is a dynamic, energizing presenter who speaks internationally to thousands each year on a wide variety of motivational and business topics. The focus of her motivational presentations includes understanding current lifestyles, design and color trends, establishing family traditions and values, balancing life through gardening principles, nurturing relationships and connections, celebrating the experiences of life, overcoming challenges, and enhancing and fostering creativity. She often incorporates flowers into her presentations. Kathy also speaks to business audiences about current trends, visual merchandising, and promotion.

She has written more than thirty-six instructional books and produced fifty flower arranging and wedding floral design instructional videos that are sold internationally. More than 1.3 million of Kathy's books have been sold.

Her television show, *Kathy Lamancusa's At Home with Flowers,* has aired on PBS stations around the United States. Kathy has also appeared as a guest on shows that air on Home & Garden Television, The Discovery Channel, The Learning Channel, TNN, CBN, CNN, and the four major networks.

She is a freelance writer and editor who works with international trade and consumer magazines providing editorial services, designs, and articles on lifestyles and color trends. She is the Trends editor for *Craftrends*/Primedia Publications.

Kathy lives with her husband, Joe, in North Canton, Ohio. When not traveling, she enjoys being at home, studying the stars from the center of her hot tub, reading while having a hot cup of tea, and walking through the garden. Her two sons, Joe and Jim, are young adults who are studying and traveling the world. Her favorite flower is the lilac, followed closely by the daisy.